WHERE TO EAT AROUND THE WORLD

TRAVEL+
LEISURE

The North Fork
Lunch Truck
in Southold,
New York.

WHERE TO
EAT
AROUND THE WORLD

Introduction by Nancy Novogrod

TRAVEL+
LEISURE
BOOKS

AMERICAN EXPRESS PUBLISHING CORPORATION
NEW YORK

Travel + Leisure
WHERE TO EAT AROUND THE WORLD

Editor Jennifer Miranda
Consulting Editors Laura Begley Bloom, Irene Edwards,
Niloufar Motamed, Clara O. Sedlak
Art Director Phoebe Flynn Rich
Photo Editor Zoey E. Klein
Consulting Photo Editor Elizabeth Boyle
Production Associate David Richey
Editorial Assistant Nate Storey
Copy Editors David Gunderson, Jane Halsey, Edward
Karam, Sarah Khan, Pablo Morales, Libby Sentz
Researchers Kyle Avallone, Judy De Young,
Tomás Martín

TRAVEL + LEISURE
Editor-in-Chief Nancy Novogrod
Design Director Sandra Garcia
Executive Editor/Content Strategist Jennifer Barr
Managing Editor Laura Teusink
Associate Managing Editor Patrick Sheehan
Arts/Research Editor Mario R. Mercado
Copy Chief Kathy Roberson
Photo Director Scott Hall
Production Manager Ayad Sinawi

AMERICAN EXPRESS PUBLISHING CORPORATION
President and Chief Executive Officer Ed Kelly
Chief Marketing Officer and President,
Digital Media Mark V. Stanich
CFO, SVP, Corporate Development and Operations
Paul B. Francis
VP, General Managers Frank Bland, Keith Strohmeier
VP, Books and Products Marshall Corey
Director, Books Programs Bruce Spanier
Senior Marketing Manager, Branded Books
Eric Lucie
Associate Marketing Manager Stacy Mallis
Director of Fulfillment and Premium Value
Philip Black
Manager of Customer Experience and Product
Development Betsy Wilson
Director of Finance Thomas Noonan
Associate Business Manager Uma Mahabir
VP, Operations Tracy Kelliher
Operations Director Anthony White

Cover: Cuc Gach Quan, in Ho Chi Minh City, Vietnam.
Photographed by Brown W. Cannon III.

Back cover, from top: A raspberry-sorbet dessert at
North Fork Table & Inn, in Southold, New York; the entrance
to Waterford Estate, in Stellenbosch, South Africa; *dakos*
(bread with tomato and feta) from Boutari Wineries,
in Crete, Greece. Photographed by Mark Mahaney (top);
DOOK (middle); Dagmar Schwelle (bottom).

Illustrated by Julia Rothman

ISBN 978-1-932624-62-5

Published by American Express Publishing Corporation
1120 Avenue of the Americas
New York, New York 10036

Distributed by Charlesbridge Publishing
85 Main Street, Watertown, Massachusetts 02472

Printed in the U.S.A.

The *bánh mì*
burger at
Bachi Burger, in
Las Vegas.

BISCOTTES

GERIE *Du Pain & Des Idées*

UR LEVAIN NATUREL

FLEUR D'ORANGER

Enjoying a croissant outside Du Pain et des Idées, in Paris.

Contents

PRICE KEY

HOTELS
$ *Less than $200*
$$ *$200 to $350*
$$$ *$350 to $500*
$$$$ *$500 to $1,000*
$$$$$ *More than $1,000*

RESTAURANTS
$ *Less than $25*
$$ *$25 to $75*
$$$ *$75 to $150*
$$$$ *More than $150*

Pescado a la talla (grilled fish with two sauces) at Contramar, in Mexico City.

Introduction

Long before the American obsession with celebrity chefs, international cuisine, and vineyards, vintages, and *terroir*, travelers were at the vanguard of culinary exploration. The delights of sampling regional flavors, trying new restaurants, and visiting markets in unfamiliar and distinctive settings are for many people reason enough to venture out into the world. This point of view hits close to home with me: shopping for spices and seasonings in Budapest, for hot sauces and condiments in Shanghai, and for jams and honey in London has yielded memories that are my own equivalents of Proust's madeleine.

Because you and so many of the readers of *Travel + Leisure* share our food obsessions, we've created *Where to Eat Around the World*, a comprehensive guide to the destinations that excite the imagination, trigger the taste buds, and challenge even the most adventurous eaters. Assembled by T+L's editors and culled from the thousands of extraordinary destinations we've featured in the magazine, this volume provides a feast of gustatory pleasures for travelers on the hunt for their next great meal, from delectable *pho* served in a hole-in-the-wall in Hanoi, Vietnam, to the best *pizza bianca* in Rome.

The stories in this book are hatched from all manner of culinary inspiration. There's a roundup of the multicultural places that are defining the dining scene in London right now, a primer on the sweets that await in Paris's *boulangeries* and patisseries, and a guide to the little-known Amazonian flavors that are landing on dinner plates in São Paulo, Brazil. But many times the best places to eat don't require a passport: we open with a tour of the mom-and-pop farm stands and seaside clam shacks in Long Island, New York's bucolic North Fork region, then take you on a three-day bender through both the outrageously rarefied and exceedingly low-key dining rooms of Las Vegas.

Also on the menu in this book: a rollicking barbecue-themed jaunt through Texas Hill Country, a journey to find the definitive bowl of ramen in its Japanese birthplace, a gonzo foray into the burgeoning (not to mention over-the-top) food scene in high-rising Dubai, and a quest for the tastiest *lechón asado* (roasted pig) in Puerto Rico, one of Le Bernardin chef Eric Ripert's favorite places to eat.

As you peruse these pages, you'll also find all the details you need to bring your own epicurean adventure to life—hotels, things to do, and restaurants, of course, but also recommendations on what to order and what to bring back home with you (after all, the packaging alone can be a lovely evocation of meals you won't soon forget). Now, who's hungry?

Nancy Novogrod EDITOR-IN-CHIEF

Pulling up to Claudio's seaside clam bar, on Long Island, New York's North Fork.

The United States

Riding the grounds at Shinn Estate Vineyards, in Mattituck, New York.

North Fork Idyll

BY MATT LEE AND TED LEE / PHOTOGRAPHED BY MARK MAHANEY

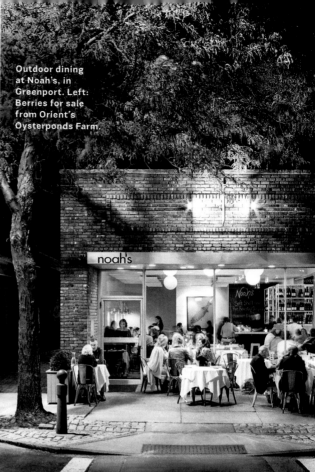

Outdoor dining at Noah's, in Greenport. Left: Berries for sale from Orient's Oysterponds Farm.

North Fork Table & Inn's striped bass with eggplant and tomato. Right: Will Lee at Sang Lee Farms, in Peconic.

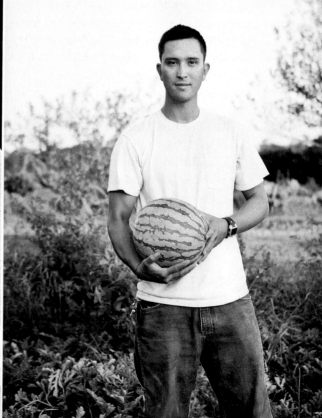

The windswept North Fork, a 30-mile-long finger of farmland between Long Island Sound and the bays that separate it from the South Fork, has two main spines of blacktop. The northern route is a highway through potato fields and vineyards. The two-lane southern road, by contrast, meanders through the farm villages of Cutchogue and Southold, and is further slowed by the fact that it just may have more farm stands per square mile than any place on earth. Roadside signage often takes the form of a ladder of hand-painted tags—TOMATOES, MELONS, DUCKS, FRESH EGGS— hanging one from another, and at the peak of summer a single farm might offer

20 different items. To read them all, drivers must slow down to a pace that infuriates anyone behind them— especially those keeping city time.

We're the kind of guys who would, by habit, crawl to a stop at every such stand, scrutinizing the baby eggplants at Sang Lee Farms, sampling peaches at Wickham's down the way. But on this clear, bright August day we were running late for a reservation at Noah's. We'd heard from friends with a summer place in Cutchogue that the restaurant does excellent work with the region's fish and shellfish and functions as a crucible for a newly energized food community of bankers turned poultry farmers, firebrand organic winemakers, and upstart purveyors of artisanal ice cream. They all channel the Slow Food ethics that have made the North Fork one of the most compelling dining destinations within reach of New York City.

Before dinner, we made a quick detour to check in at the Silver Sands, a no-frills but tidy motel-with-cabins near the town of Greenport that harks back to a golden age of Long Island summering: a neon marquee from the 1960's, a framed needlepoint Welcome sign at the front desk, and a crescent of beach hugging a cove where you could imagine whiling away a weekend or a lifetime.

After dropping off our bags and taking a perfunctory dip in the water, we hustled to Greenport, the maritime village that's the commercial center of the North Fork, and to Noah's. The terrace was packed; the lofty dining room buzzing with a crowd of regulars.

A table of ladies with silvery coifs cooed over their waiter (who happened to be the grandson of one of them) while a weekending family, toddlers in tow, feasted on crab tacos and Gorgonzola-and-rosemary fries. We took our seats at the bar and in short order had glasses of crisp Chenin Blanc from Paumonok, a winery we'd passed not 20 minutes ago, and an iced platter of local oysters: Hogs Neck, Blue Point, and the alluringly named Pipes Cove.

"Where's Pipes Cove?" we asked the bartender.

"Know where the Sands Motel is?" she said. "Right out front."

The following morning, the innkeeper confirmed it: his cousin's oyster beds are just beyond the motel's swimming area.

"Sometimes you get a stray from the pens," he said. "You can feel them with your toes."

You'd be hard-pressed to find a more instantly immersive foodscape than the North Fork in summertime. Being a locavore is less an identity here than a fact of existence on a peninsula where so much of the land is given over to growing food and where the waters yield such astonishingly large amounts of fresh fish and shellfish. For more than 200 years, the region has been a breadbasket for New York City, and you see it everywhere, written into the very geography: the neighboring villages of Orient and East Marion were known as "Oysterponds" in the 19th century.

While the North Fork and nearby Shelter Island have been summer communities for New York City families since the Victorian era, and a nascent wine-making industry has more recently attracted travelers and new residents, we were drawn here because the area's agricultural and maritime traditions have preserved it from becoming an extension of the South Fork, so easily lampooned in the catfights that can break out over a parking space. Or worse, from suffering the fate of Montauk, where the influx of a well-heeled creative class, limited-edition Marc Jacobs surfboards under their arms, has turned the barefoot-beachy idyll into a hipster cliché seemingly overnight. The North Fork is still a fedora-free zone, where artists mix it up with oystermen and bikers with blue bloods; the most coveted item of jewelry is a sailor's-knot bracelet.

On our way back to Greenport, we pulled off the main road when we passed a sign for Oysterponds Farm, with hand-drawn illustrations advertising blueberries, red raspberries, and yellow raspberries. But we found no raspberries on display, only pint after pint of plump blueberries.

"Is raspberry season over?" we asked the older gentleman minding the stand.

"Heavens, no," he said. "We had plenty this morning—yellow and red—but we're all out now. If you had'na slept in...."

After we bought some blueberries, he elaborated: typically, the pickers might head out for another harvest pass if they ran out, but the fields today were already too hot for the health of the workers.

The North Fork undeniably moves to the rhythm of farm life, and there's a wry resistance to the vicissitudes of Mother Nature and the control she exerts. The climate here is capricious, from day to day—and year upon year. Which means wine making on the North Fork is for only the bravest. If American appellations like Napa and Sonoma tend to romanticize the pleasures of wine making, Long Island emphatically does not. No, sir. These folks are *honest*, and if you ever thought owning a winery might be an amusing, laird-of-the-manor retirement pursuit, we'd suggest you sign up for the weekly wine newsletter David Page sends out from his Shinn Estate Vineyards and become acquainted with every pest, every mold spore, and the nail-biting

realities: behind each sun-washed day in Mattituck might be a morning of gale-force winds and pelting hail.

Once you've read about the battles Page faces every day to make the vineyards sustainable, as we did, you'll be inclined to visit the vineyard to see for yourself. At seven o'clock on a Friday evening, the tasting terrace was at full tilt, and a clutch of bridesmaids were drinking rosé and getting their palms read by the in-house psychic. We tasted glasses of the winery's exuberant Coalescence, a spicy and suave blend of Chardonnay, Sauvignon Blanc, and Riesling, watching the setting sun cast the clouds pinker and pinker still in a bright blue bowl of sky.

We were tempted to linger late into the evening, but dinner at the North Fork Table & Inn beckoned. Here, we found the early riser who'd cleaned Oysterponds out of their berries. It was Claudia Fleming, who is the dean of the new North Fork dining scene along with her husband, Gerry Hayden, a Long Island native. Seasoned Manhattan veterans (she was pastry chef at Gramercy Tavern during Tom Colicchio's heyday; he was sous-chef at Charlie Palmer's Aureole), they decamped for Southold in 2006 and freshened up an old

inn and tavern into an elegant restaurant with rooms. The cooking is seasonal and focused: a meaty Long Island duck breast with perfect crisped fat and buttery chanterelles; a Block Island fluke *crudo* with ruby grapefruit. The stunner of the night was the summer berry meringue sandwich—tart red-raspberry ice cream sandwiched between two crisp meringue cookies and surrounded by those Oysterponds red and yellow raspberries, so sweet and floral, as delicate as jasmine. We were grateful we hadn't missed them.

f one of the joys of the North Fork is celebrating its being the "Un-Hamptons," another side of the quiet community's life is looking out for signs that it might be getting "too crowded," "too social," or "too flashy." Shopkeepers and waiters in Greenport roll their eyes and shrug when tourists ask if they know who owns the enormous yachts and speedboats that occasionally dock at the city marina. A friend who recently bought a house in the sleepy, easternmost village of Orient warily told us the local general store had been bought by twentysomethings from the Berkshires and that the scene there could get a little "intense."

When we went to check it out, however, things were decidedly low-key. One owner, Grayson Murphy, was noodling around on a guitar on the front porch. His wife, Miriam Foster, was inside, having just pulled a sheet of freshly baked chocolate chip cookies from the oven. We bagged up a few, then popped next door to the Idle Hour, an ice cream shop run by the precocious 20-year-old Rosy Brown. If you're trying to escape city life, finding out that Brown is the daughter of prominent Manhattan art dealer Gavin Brown might be too close for comfort (the I SCREAM T-shirts she sells are by Argentine international art star Rirkrit Tiravanija). But then she's grown up in both worlds and, as such, caters to both, offering two brands of ice cream: the Brooklyn cult label Blue Marble for the yoga-mat-toting city folk, and Hershey's for the rest of us. We ordered Hershey's vanilla sundaes with house-made caramel sauce, perched ourselves on a bench on the front porch of the shop, crumbled our chocolate chip cookies over the top, and finished our sundaes before a single car passed by.

West of Orient, Greenport gets the lion's share of the tourist throngs most summer weekends with ferry traffic from Shelter Island and visitors from New York City. But even on its busiest days, the town retains a down-home anticommercial feel in keeping with the spirit of the farm villages of Cutchogue and Southold to the west, with their honor-jar vegetable concessions and hand-lettered signs. There's a well-stocked marine-supply store and an antiques shop selling authentic regional finds: weathered burlap potato sacks printed with the names of bygone North Fork farms and clam rakes that have seen dozens of seasons of service.

And then there's Aldo's. Several years ago, North Fork denizens drew a collective, horrified gasp when a Starbucks opened in Greenport near Aldo's, a coffee shop presided over by the mercurial, curmudgeonly Aldo Maiorana, a Sicilian roaster-barista with a mad-scientist halo of silver curls who's been pulling espresso in the area for almost 30 years. Maiorana responded by moving his operation directly across the street from the Starbucks, which only seemed to raise the stakes; after all, as many people as there are who love Aldo's coffee, there are an equal number who find it bitter (although few seem to quibble about the buttery-crisp scones). And as generations of local teenagers who have been employed at Aldo's can attest, Maiorana's demeanor has proved no less divisive. He reduced a friend of ours to tears with a lecture on the correct way to sweep a floor when she worked for him in the nineties.

But this is the North Fork. Five years on, the Starbucks has closed. And whenever the Italian-*tricolore* "Open" flag waves at Aldo's, the scent of warm scones hovers over a slow-moving line of customers that stretches from the espresso machine to the front door. Outside, a bitterly aromatic fog of roasting coffee beans wafts over the town green.

Down on the docks, the Greenport restaurant scene is dominated by Claudio's, a small empire with a 143-year history. The flagship, Claudio's, with its acres of mahogany and marble and old-school service, appeals to a more traditional, graying crowd. Outdoors are the two livelier establishments in the chain, each separated by a channel. Crabby Jerry's, a pick-up window for steamed lobsters and clam rolls, is on one dock, and on another is Claudio's Clam Bar, the clear crowd favorite, attracting motorcycle and car clubs looking for sustenance on their Sunday drives. When we arrived at opening time, at

Raspberry sorbet with fresh fruit at North Fork Table & Inn. Below: Shinn Estate Vineyards' tasting patio.

11:30 a.m. on the dot, a Harley Motorcycle Club and a Dodge Viper Car Club had already turned the parking lot into an impromptu show of gawkers.

Out under the tent on the dock is the pulse of the Clam Bar scene: the raucous car clubs, round tables of families, and couples tucking in to bowls of steamed clams in white wine and methodically breaking down lobsters from Crabby Jerry's. Shortly after being seated, we heard the throaty growl of a speedboat drifting ever so slowly into the narrow channel, its pilot chomping a cigar, deeply concentrating on berthing the boat alongside the dock of the Clam Bar. Minutes later, another. And then another. Our waitress explained that this was the drill every weekend, the ballet of cigarette boats tying up three deep in the channel.

We ate light—a quick platter of clams on the half shell washed down with ice-cold Roanoke rosé—because we were meeting friends at a restaurant that had just opened a few docks west of where we were. They said the owner of the well-regarded Vine Street Café, on Shelter Island, had taken over the local chowder dive and remade it into Blue Canoe Oyster Bar & Grill. So we walked across the harborfront to find our dining companions—with a stop to gawk at the *Milk & Honey*, a 125-foot yacht moored at the city dock, its crew in matching polos and shorts hustling around the boat.

A whitewashed post-and-beam tavern room with a plummy nautical décor, the Blue Canoe has a generous terrace overlooking a boardwalk linking the less-trafficked part of the harborfront east of the Shelter Island Ferry dock to the town green. The matching orange umbrellas and boatsman's livery of the waitstaff brought to mind the outdoor lounges of Miami or St. Bart's. A smart, summery menu of lobster rolls, with a great raw bar sourced locally, had the resolutely new-school inflections of a globe-trotting chef: tuna *tataki*; *chimichurri* mayo; chili-lime shrimp.

In the strip of beach just beyond the terrace, a small seaplane was casually tied up, and the diners and pedestrians on the boardwalk were doing their best to appear nonchalant. At least until the passengers, a party of four sitting a few tables away, got up to leave and walked toward the beach. They stepped gingerly onto the pontoons and up into the cockpit one by one. And when they were all in, the pilot fired up the engine, the propeller's backdraft causing the plantings around the boardwalk to shudder, and they puttered out toward the boat traffic in the harbor.

We lost sight of the plane as it angled out around a dock, and turned back to our bluefish tacos and pulled-pork sandwiches. But a minute later, people walking along the harborfront began moving toward the docks to watch the plane take off. We wondered aloud at the table whether Blue Canoe would become the new Sunset Beach, just across the water on Shelter Island, with seaplanes jostling for positions out front like the cigarette boats. While it's too early to tell, it did seem in that instant as the plane lofted above the harbor and all eyes—waitstaff; diners; the crew on the deck of the *Milk & Honey*—watched the plane soar above the harbor, arcing up and away and finally out of sight, that we were witnessing the dawning of a new era in this old maritime village. ✦

GUIDE

New York City

Where are in-the-know New Yorkers eating now? The answers are as varied as the city's latest dining trends. Witness the multipurpose spaces, equal parts grocery store and restaurant; the artisanal cafés with urban gardens; the Brooklyn-bred chef's tables drawing Manhattanites across the river. Care to join them? Here, nine places that are defining the city's culinary landscape.

ABC Kitchen by Jean-Georges

Chef Dan Kluger captures the locavore zeitgeist with a menu to make Californians swoon: a whole-wheat pizza with Jersey tomatoes and milky buffalo mozzarella; kale salad sharpened by serrano chiles, lemon, and mint; and Maine lobster roasted in the wood oven. All this in a space most cramped city dwellers wish was their living room. *35 E. 18th St.; 212/475-5829; abckitchennyc.com.* **$$$**

Calliope

NYC's *bistronomie* movement got a kick start with the opening of Ginevra Iverson and Eric Korsh's downtown bistro. The braised rabbit legs are tossed with eggy pappardelle and white wine, and halibut comes on peppery *romesco* toast in a saffron mussel broth. French wine and gracious service complete the picture. *84 E. Fourth St.; 212/260-8484; calliopenyc.com.* **$$$**

Chef's Table at Brooklyn Fare

On an otherwise bland block, the Michelin three-starred Chef's Table at Brooklyn Fare has become one of the city's most coveted tables (reservations are taken Mondays at 10:30 a.m. for six weeks out). At the center of an 18-seat, stainless-steel bar, César Ramírez conjures up some 20 courses each night, a seafood-centric cavalcade (Kumamoto oysters; jalapeño langoustines) with elegant trimmings, such as Iranian caviar and gold-leaf ribbons. *200 Schermerhorn St., Brooklyn; 718/243-0050; brooklynfare.com.* **$$$$**

Il Buco Alimentari & Vineria

This of-the-moment operation channels New Yorkers' love of multitasking. A café, a bakery, and a provisions shop in the front dispense espresso, house-cured salumi, and sea salts for takeout; in the back, the dining area serves Italian favorites, including *bucatini cacio e pepe* and *porchetta*. *53 Great Jones St.; 212/837-2622; ilbucovineria.com.* **$$$**

The NoMad

At the forefront of the hotel restaurant renaissance is the NoMad, from Daniel Humm and Will Guidara, the team behind Eleven Madison Park. In an elegant room with velvety seats and crimson drapes, Chef Humm offers a rustic take on French-inspired dishes such as whole chicken roasted in an open hearth. The library bar is an imbibing bibliophile's dream; order a Satan's Circus, made with rye whiskey and chile-infused Aperol. *1170 Broadway; 212/796-1500; thenomadhotel.com.* **$$$**

Pok Pok Phat Thai

Vermont native Andy Ricker fell for the techniques of northwest Thailand, then conquered the Portland, Oregon, food scene. Who better to raise the bar (and spice level) of Thai cooking in NYC? Visit his low-key noodle bar in Manhattan, where the authentic pad thai is made with tamarind, fish sauce, and a hint of chili. Or head to the Brooklyn outpost for Chiang Mai sausage with Burmese curry powder. *137 Rivington St.; 212/477-1299; pokpokphatthai.com.* **$$**

Red Rooster Harlem

When the Ethiopian-born Swedish chef Marcus Samuelsson bought a house in Harlem, he knew his neighborhood needed a watering hole worthy of its storied past. Enter Red Rooster, a lively spot that specializes in multiculti comfort food (cured meats with lingonberry jam; fried "yardbird"). *310 Lenox Ave.; 212/792-9001; redroosterharlem.com.* **$$$**

Roberta's

Hop the L train to a cinder-block warehouse in Bushwick for a taste of the Neapolitan pizzas that have launched a thousand foodie blog posts. Carlo Mirarchi crafts ethereal pies that are seasoned with ingredients picked from the restaurant's garden. Behind Roberta's, Mirarchi has also opened Blanca, a sleek tasting room where the seafood menu may include horse mackerel, soft-shell crabs, or perch. *261 Moore St., Brooklyn; 718/417-1118; robertaspizza.com and blancanyc.com.* **$$$**

Torrisi Italian Specialties

It's the flagship that started a traditional-Italian empire. The always-changing small-plates menu (fusilli with duck *ragù*; monkfish *oreganata*) at Rich Torrisi and Mario Carbone's SoHo hot spot is a paean to the flavors of the Lower East Side. Next door, Parm delivers when it comes to expertly made deli sandwiches. And at their 1950's-style trattoria Carbone, the duo have perfected the red-sauce-joint concept with updated classics such as lobster fra diavolo. *250 Mulberry St.; 212/965-0955; torrisinyc.com.* **$$$$**

César Ramírez applying the finishing touches at Chef's Table. Right: Pok Pok Phat Thai's Chiang Mai sausage.

Cured meats at Il Buco Alimentari & Vineria. Left: Café seating outside Red Rooster Harlem.

Your Big Fat Las Vegas Food Adventure

BY PETER JON LINDBERG
PHOTOGRAPHED BY CORAL VON ZUMWALT

Kobe beef, duck, and vegetable skewers at Aburiya Raku. Opposite: Twin Elvis impersonators stop to pose on the Strip.

Vegas inspires a person to do crazy things. Like, say, eat your way through the city's best dishes— *robata* to Rajasthani, haute French to French toast—in a four-day restaurant binge. Are you ready?

DAY 1 You arrive after lunchtime, having eaten only half a bag of pretzel nuggets on the plane ride in. You are famished. Jack is surveying his notes. He has a list of 47 restaurants and less than 79 hours to attempt to try them all.

This absurd stunt was his idea. Jack is a foodie's foodie, possessed of boundless appetites and an ironclad liver. He has 2,987 Chowhound posts. He reads Menupages in bed. But this is too big a task for one, so he's coaxed you along as his wingman. Together you will devour the daylights out of the culinary candyland that is Las Vegas, Nevada.

There is ground to cover. Vegas is no longer defined by splashy casino-side restaurants, though there are still plenty of those. For food lovers the parameters have expanded tenfold: to off-Strip ramen joints, far-flung suburban pizzerias, chef's haunts in Chinatown mini-malls.

You have packed Excedrin, Maalox, Lipitor. By Thursday you will have consumed 19 pounds of shellfish, 22 liters of booze, five lobes of foie gras, 15 sticks of butter, and three micrograms of edible gold leaf. The only thing that really worries you is the foie. There is nothing more depraved than a man in the depths of a foie gras binge.

Jack slides behind the wheel of the rental car. You take a deep breath and open the passenger door.
3:09 p.m. Archi's Thai Kitchen You are in a stucco hut across from a pet-grooming service. You would not have glanced twice at this place had a chef friend of

Jack's not steered you here. You surely wouldn't have guessed that Archi's would serve the best chicken *satay* of your life, a life now steeped in regret over not having found it sooner: tender thigh meat marinated overnight in curry powder, sugar, and garlic, deep-fried and then grilled to an ideal balance of juiciness and char. Most *satay* sauces are peanut-buttery sweet, but this is spicy, dusky, demanding another dip.

While Jack talks Thai to the waitstaff, you scan the listings in *Las Vegas Weekly*: Manilow, Rod Stewart, Donny & Marie. You have found a secret portal to 1976!
4:44 p.m. Bachi Burger You are heading south. Rumor has it there's a spot out beyond the airport specializing in pork buns and Asian-inflected burgers.

Bachi's menu reads as if Harold and Kumar are in the kitchen doing bong hits. Of the six whacked-out burgers on offer, the highlight is an homage to the Vietnamese *bánh mì*, blending beef, pork, shrimp, and pork pâté with pickled carrots and daikon. Fresh lemongrass, mint, and basil add brightness, while fish

Chef Mitsou Endo, owner of Aburiya Raku, holding a yellowtail. Left: Fremont Street, in downtown Las Vegas.

sauce supplies depth. It is intensely satisfying. Jack orders a third.

5:36 p.m. CityCenter You have booked rooms at the Mandarin Oriental, because you're not the type of people who open drapes by hand. Here, a single control panel will ring your alarm and automatically raise the curtains, jack up the A/C, and switch on the *Today* show. Downside: it takes 17 minutes to figure out the shower.

The Mandarin is one of three hotels in the CityCenter complex, whose gimmick is having no gimmick. It is no pyramid or castle or volcano, but a simulacrum of a sleek Modernist metropolis, designed by name architects (Libeskind, Pelli), complete with art installations (Rauschenberg, Stella) and real-live pedestrians. "Modernistan" would've been a better name.

6:41 p.m. Julian Serrano You're at the Aria Resort & Casino, where most of Modernistan's restaurants are located. Dinner (round one) is at Julian Serrano's tapas restaurant. Serrano is the chef behind Picasso at the Bellagio. You have high hopes. Just as a bistro can

be judged by its *poulet rôti*, a tapas bar is only as good as its *pan tomate*. "And its sangria," Jack adds. Both arrive swiftly. The *pan tomate*, rafts of toasted bread rubbed with tomato, garlic, and grassy olive oil, is terrific; the sangria overly sweet but functional. Jack summons a platter of blistered Padrón peppers sprinkled with sea salt. With his eyes glued on the Anne Hathaway ringer at the hostess stand, he whistles along as the stereo blasts "Centerfold."

8:18 p.m. Sage After a pitcher of saccharine sangria, you stroll over to Sage, back at CityCenter. Chef Shawn McClain made his name at Spring and Green Zebra, in Chicago. Sage hews to the same farm-to-table approach—or, in Vegas's case, FedEx-to-table. You assume two leather-clad stools at the bar. Jack's food-critic pal has recommended the foie gras crème brûlée. It sounds ridiculous. Laced with cocoa nibs and bing cherries, spiked with brandy and Grand Marnier, it is, in fact, ridiculously good. Your bartender, who's pairing beers with each dish, sets down two glasses of

Joël Robuchon's Le Caviar, made with crab meat and fennel cream. Left: Circus Circus at night.

Eating a sashimi salad at Raku. Right: A pitcher of sangria from Julian Serrano.

Dogfish Head's Midas Touch—more mead than ale, redolent of saffron and muscat grapes. A yellowtail *crudo,* incongruously plated with black truffles and trumpet mushrooms, turns out to be a brilliant mix of ethereal and earthy, ocean and forest floor. You stumble outside and hail a cab to the Wynn.

10:05 p.m. **Bartolotta Ristorante di Mare** Most people would be done for the night. Most would not be at Paul Bartolotta's coastal-Italian restaurant for Dinner No. 3. Most people aren't you and Jack. You would've preferred to sit in a cabana by the faux lagoon outside. Instead, you're relegated to a two-top by the bar, where you're assaulted by schmaltzy ballads. Bartolotta is known for impeccably fresh and shockingly expensive fish, most of it line-caught (very eco-friendly) and flown in every other day from Italy (very not). Your waiter rolls up a cart full of evidence: silver-flecked sea bream; spiny scorpion fish; glistening snapper that two nights ago was swimming off the Ligurian coast. You can choose any fish to be grilled or roasted. For an extra $85, the waiter says, the kitchen will shave white truffles on anything. ("Feh," Jack says. "I know a girl who'll do that for $25.") You settle on the snapper.

A flurry of starters materializes: marinated anchovies; baby clams sautéed with white wine, tomato, and garlic; Sicilian saber fish that's charcoal-grilled and rightfully left alone. The Ligurian octopus is so tender you slice it with a butter knife. The waiter explains that it was massaged "exactly 500 times," which inspires some speculation about whose job that is and how one might describe it on a résumé. At last comes the snapper, which requires nothing more than a splash of olive oil, a squeeze of lemon, and a few quick minutes on the grill.

When the bill arrives it's past midnight and you're well past coherent, reeling from omega-3's, wine, and bad Italian disco. Jack is raring for a nightcap and soup dumplings. "It's 1 a.m.!" he brays. "Do you know where your inner children are?!?"

DAY 2 You passed out in your trousers. Soup dumplings were a terrible idea. When Al Roker appears and the curtains slide open to an angry sun, you're cotton-mouthed and unsure of your whereabouts. You squint out the window for clues: Egypt? Monte Carlo? The head spins. A $14 bowl of oatmeal hardly helps.

Over breakfast at the Mandarin, Jack plots out the day's meals.

12:20 p.m. **Settebello Pizzeria Napoletana** First up: a Neapolitan pizza parlor in the nearby suburb of Green Valley. Settebello is equipped with a 950-degree wood-fired oven perfect for blistering the crust just so. Your brain feels like a 950-degree oven. Your companion is mysteriously unaffected. While you wait for your pies, bright-eyed Jack chats up the *pizzaiolo.* Like any respectable Italian, he uses Molina Caputo flour to ensure a chewy, slightly sour crust. Atop the margherita he adds San Marzano tomatoes, olive oil, Parmigiano-Reggiano, mozzarella, and basil. The result is damn impressive. After two slices you have regained your peripheral vision.

4:03 p.m. **Origin India Restaurant & Bar** Somewhere between stops at Hot N Juicy Crawfish and a north-side *molcajetes* stand, your hangover subsided. Now you're at Origin India, double-fisting ice water and a 20-ounce Taj Mahal. With its Moghul archways and amiable staff, Origin is a cut above the typical South Asian restaurant. You could make a fine meal from the street-snacks menu alone: the *bhel puri* (puffed rice, potatoes, and onions in tamarind sauce) is as tasty as any you've had in Mumbai. You tear into plush naan with wild mushrooms and truffle oil, savory biryani, and a phenomenal *rogan josh* made with New Zealand lamb shank. Fully restored, you cross the street to the Hard Rock for a round of blackjack. Your dealer is an amiable Filipino named Wilson, like the volleyball. With two large riding on the bet, he cajoles you into splitting a pair of eights. You bust. *Wilson!!!*

8:16 p.m. **Joël Robuchon** At last, here you are: the grandest restaurant in Vegas, from the man some call the world's greatest chef. Joël Robuchon is located at the MGM Grand, though it does its best not to appear so: guests are picked up by limousine, delivered to a private entrance of the MGM's exclusive Mansion annex, and escorted through a series of rear corridors, *Goodfellas*-style, to the sumptuous, 50-seat dining room. Swathed in regal purples and golds, the interior is like a set from *Die Zauberflöte.* Surprisingly, it is the furthest thing from stiff. Laughter mingles with the bright tinkle of jazz piano. Your table is covered in what appear to be Mardi Gras beads.

A bread cart emerges, and you begin to giggle. It is the Maybach of bread carts, laden with saffron focaccia, Gruyère brioche, olive flutes—plus a nearly five-pound slab of butter, flown in from Brittany, that reminds you what real butter tastes like.

Robuchon's 16-course tasting menu costs $425 a person. (You are down that much at blackjack. Jack is treating.) As at so many Michelin three-stars, the opening courses are the standouts, their daintiness and concision whispering a whole evening's worth of promise: a tin of osetra caviar hiding a layer of crabmeat and fennel cream; airy egg-yolk ravioli with chanterelles and spinach foam. Pairings are equally assured. A minerally white Burgundy from Méo-Camuzet drinks beautifully with roasted lobster and sea-urchin flan.

Vegas is no longer defined by splashy casino-side restaurants, though there are still plenty of those. For food lovers the parameters have expanded tenfold.

At some point you are no longer consuming food; food is consuming you. Time has stopped. Before you know it a *mignardises* cart appears, glittering like a jewel box. Is it really 12:15? The four-hour bacchanal has left you strangely energized, the way great Japanese food does. Your feet feel lighter as you stride to the casino for some postprandial Texas Hold'em.

You win a few hands. You could play more. But the night is young, Jack insists, and—speaking of Japanese—Raku is just getting started.

2:07 a.m. Aburiya Raku You are not the kind of person who would be at a place like this at this time of the morning. Then again, nobody goes to Raku before midnight. Certainly not the chefs who make up much of the restaurant's clientele. (Hey, isn't that Paul Bartolotta?)

Tucked in a strip mall on Spring Mountain Road, the heart of Vegas's Chinatown, Raku shot to cult status soon after opening in 2008. The focus is on *robata*—charcoal-grilled meats, fish, and vegetables—but the real treats are on the daily-changing chalkboard menu: pristine fried prawns; quivering cubes of house-made tofu; a velvety poached egg with Santa Barbara sea urchin; silky custard with silkier foie gras. This is hearty Japanese soul food, ideally paired with sake or beer. (The faux-hawked barman suggests Ginga Kogen, an unfiltered hefeweizen from Nishiwaga.) You wind up closing the place down, staggering out as the staff are stacking the chairs.

DAY 3 When you awake, the *Today* show is long over. Housekeeping has given up and left a note. You're bloodshot, bleary-eyed, and ravenous. You could murder some French toast. Your cohort knows just the place.
12:41 p.m. Peppermill Restaurant & Fireside Lounge Uh-oh. You've heard about the Peppermill. About its monstrous breakfasts and giant Scorpion Bowls (both served 24/7); the fake trees foresting the dining room; the goofy fire pits dating to the Carter administration.

For once, notoriety is inadequate. Your waitress wears a dress so low-cut the neckline catches on her belly ring. She brings you Bloody Marys the size of Big Gulps. The French Toast Collage includes not only a seven-inch stack of battered challah but three fried eggs, bacon, sausage, and several golf balls of whipped butter. You are impervious to pain, cholesterol, remorse.
2:53 p.m. Monta *"Irasshaimase!"* shout the cooks as you enter. They're wearing do-rags and white rubber boots. You take the only two empty seats. The other 24 are occupied entirely by Japanese: hipsters, businessmen, hipster-businessmen, and an octogenarian in a trilby. Just two doors down from Raku, Monta specializes in *tonkotsu* ramen, a nutty pork broth of unfathomable depth, laden with wood-ear mushrooms, scallions, and a boiled egg. To this bowl of id you have added strips of roast pork belly that dissolve on the tongue. Your blood runs several degrees warmer as you slurp the last spoonful.

Spring Mountain Road resembles any suburban miracle mile, except every storefront has a pagoda roof. You stroll east in the fading afternoon light, Jack darting in and out of *pho* shops, *boba* tea shops, Hawaiian *poke*

Monta's *tonkotsu* ramen. Below: The alfresco dining room at Bartolotta.

joints, Macanese bakeries, Taiwanese noodle houses, and Mongolian BBQ's, snacking as you go.

7:02 p.m. Twist A nap restores your appetite. Jack has spent the interim waist-deep in a martini glass at the Golden Steer. He knocks on your door clad in Armani and apparently no worse for wear. You ascend to the Mandarin's 23rd floor and slide into a banquette at Twist, the first stateside restaurant from French chef Pierre Gagnaire.

Where Robuchon went plush, Twist goes spare, bordering on ascetic. Tiny globe pendants, flickering like distant planets, hang from a double-height ceiling. The room's pale, chilly lighting is more suited to a museum—or a spaceship. This is not a place to propose.

Gagnaire's cooking is quirky and cerebral, which doesn't mean it can't be fun. The amuse-bouche: shards of cumin flatbread to dip into tuna-infused Chantilly, then into a ramekin of dehydrated shrimp that crackle like Rice Krispies upon contact with the cream. "How cool is that?" Jack chortles, repeating the trick over and over until the waiter removes the bowl. More martinis are procured. Each course includes three separate dishes on three separate plates, which may be two too many for a man in Jack's condition. He's unsure which to tackle first: the foie gras–and-fig terrine, studded with Sauternes-soaked apricots and cosseted in speck? The rhubarb-and-eggplant mousse? Or the bracing salad of pickled chanterelles, pickled onions, and mâche, drizzled in beet syrup?

Once again, the meal peaks early. *Hamachi* ceviche is served on a chicory-and-grapefruit salad so brassy and bitter it overwhelms the fish; poached cod is buried in a cloying reduction. By the fourth course you've lost interest. "Maybe they'll bring us more Rice Krispie shrimp," Jack wonders aloud.

12:45 a.m. Society Café You shouldn't. You needn't. But: another round. A taxi whisks you to the Encore resort, where Society Café dishes out late-night comfort food. After that heady dinner, you're craving the unfussy nourishment that can only be delivered by a bowl of soup—in this case, roasted tomato bisque, with a salad of Rosso Bruno tomatoes and creamy, tangy *burrata*. From your perch at the bar, you play Spot-the-Call-Girl, Guess-the-John. Jack orders another Sazerac; you wander off to find the gents'. In the next stall a guy

Terrace dining at Joël Robuchon. Left: The chef's bone marrow and vegetable ragoût.

is chatting on the phone and, judging from the sound of plastic on porcelain, chopping rails of coke.

When did the night become a Jay McInerney novel?

DAY 4 The scale in your hotel bathroom says you've gained six pounds since Monday.

11:29 a.m. Lotus of Siam Another day, another parking lot. This one is particularly derelict— probably hosts pit-bull fights after dark. Right now its only occupants are a dozen souls queued outside a still-locked door, waiting for lunch to begin.

You've read the decade-old *Gourmet* article proclaiming Lotus of Siam "the best Thai restaurant in North America." You've heard about its branch in Manhattan, a rare case of reverse Vegas-NYC migration. You've heard the hype, and, frankly, you're determined not to buy it.

And then you finally lift fork to mouth and taste Lotus's Issan-style deep-fried beef jerky—*beef jerky* for the love of Mike!—and your eyes actually well up, not so much from the heat, though it packs plenty, as from the

sheer abundant goodness of the thing. Beneath a crackly exterior, dark as night and dusted with lemongrass, the beef is resoundingly juicy, each bite releasing waves of earthy flavor. You and Jack stare at your plates, dumbstruck. "Whoa," he murmurs. "Whoa," you reply.

4:20 p.m. Luv-It Frozen Custard While Jack goes off in search of ribs and empanadas, you manage to shed another $170 at the Aria's casino. This prompts a solo visit to Luv-It Frozen Custard, which has lifted the spirits of People-Who-Lose-at-Blackjack since Robert Goulet was headlining the Sands. You devour your sundae on the blazing-hot hood of your car. It does the trick.

With its homey façade and primitive sign, Luv-It reminds you of a bygone Las Vegas, before Wolfgang Puck arrived to make the city safe for celebrity chefs and serious dining. Since then, goes the logic, Vegas has become a bona fide food town.

Or has it? For all the great meals you've had, ambitious cooking remains very much the exception here. This is still the land of soggy pancakes and leathery steaks, of flavorless crab legs and tasteless

design. A place where restaurants offer to "add lobster to any dish—$26!" (Because who *wouldn't* want lobster in their mac and cheese?) In every other aspect of Vegas life, kitsch and silliness are fundamental. But it's hard to eat with your tongue in your cheek.

7:18 p.m. Caesars Palace The last meal is upon you. There's an 11:30 red-eye to catch. You and Jack are wrestling with a dilemma. You have a table booked upstairs at Restaurant Guy Savoy— meaning you have the chance to eat three dinners, on three consecutive nights, by three of France's greatest living chefs.

But to be honest, you are craving pasta something fierce. And just downstairs from Guy Savoy is...Rao's. Rao's! Whose 10 tables in Harlem are still the toughest booking in New York, 115 years on. And here it is in Caesars Palace, overflowing with marinara sauce and the whoops of wine-soaked celebrants. And *there's a booth available!* You marvel at the absurdity of the choice: Guy Savoy...or Rao's! Only in Vegas. So which will it be?

7:19 p.m. Rao's The Vegas outpost is four times larger than Manhattan's, but it's divided into separate dining rooms, each scaled like the original. There's a warmth here that's hard to quarrel with: soft-glowing sconces,

burnished plank floors, the obligatory head shot. Waitstaff are prone to laughter; even the busboys slap your back. Rao's inspires confidence. This is a place where, when they offer grated Parmesan, you say, "Yes," and when they offer another bottle, you say, "Hell, yes."

You say "Hell, yes" to a lot at Rao's. To a zesty *insalata di mare*—calamari, shrimp, lobster, and sweet crabmeat. To *penne alla vodka* and toothsome *fiocchetti* stuffed with ricotta and pear, in a sage-butter sauce with dried cranberries. "*That's* my jam!" shouts Jack, knocking over his wine glass. You realize how much you've missed this kind of food. (Except the meatballs. Biting into Rao's *polpette* is like gnawing on a Birkenstock.)

More wine is brought. You try to find the bathroom and wind up on the bocce court. When you return, the woman in the next booth is giving her consort a lap dance. Bombed on Barolo and cheesecake, you and Jack defer your departure. JetBlue can wait. Instead, you're hatching plans for your own casino resort. Jack's idea: Vegas, Vegas. Scale models of all the hotels on the Strip, each with just one room. "*Very* exclusive," he reasons.

"What'll the restaurants serve?" you ask.

"Small plates, of course." ✚

GUIDE

STAY

Mandarin Oriental
3752 Las Vegas Blvd. S.;
888/881-9578;
mandarinoriental.com. $

EAT

Aburiya Raku
5030 W. Spring Mountain Rd.;
702/367-3511;
raku-grill.com. $$

Archi's Thai Kitchen
6360 W. Flamingo Rd.;
702/880-5550;
archithai.com. $

Bachi Burger
470 E. Windmill Lane;
702/242-2244;
bachiburger.com. $$

Bartolotta Ristorante di Mare
Wynn Las Vegas,

3131 Las Vegas Blvd. S.;
702/770-9966;
wynnlasvegas.com. $$$$

Hot N Juicy Crawfish
4810 Spring Mountain Rd.;
702/891-8889;
hotnjuicycrawfish.com. $$

Joël Robuchon
MGM Grand Hotel & Casino,
3799 Las Vegas Blvd. S.;
702/891-7925;
mgmgrand.com. $$$$$

Julian Serrano
Aria Resort & Casino,
3730 Las Vegas Blvd. S.;
877/230-2742;
arialasvegas.com. $$$

Lotus of Siam
953 E. Sahara Ave.;
702/735-3033;
saipinchutima.com. $$

Luv-It Frozen Custard
505 E. Oakey Blvd.;
702/384-6452;
luvitfrozencustard.com. $

Monta
5030 Spring Mountain Rd.;
702/367-4600;
montaramen.com. $$

Origin India Restaurant & Bar
4480 Paradise Rd.;
702/734-6342;
originindiarestaurant.com. $$

Peppermill Restaurant & Fireside Lounge
2985 Las Vegas Blvd. S.;
702/735-4177;
peppermilllasvegas.com. $$

Rao's
Caesars Palace,
3570 Las Vegas Blvd. S.;

877/346-4642;
caesarspalace.com. $$$

Sage
Aria Resort & Casino, 3730
Las Vegas Blvd. S.; 877/230-
2742; arialasvegas.com. $$$

Settebello Pizzeria Napoletana
140 Green Valley Pkwy.,
Henderson; 702/222-3556;
settebello.net. $$

Society Café
Encore at Wynn Las Vegas,
3131 Las Vegas Blvd. S.;
702/770-5300;
wynnlasvegas.com. $$$

Twist by Pierre Gagnaire
Mandarin Oriental,
3752 Las Vegas Blvd. S.;
888/881-9578;
mandarinoriental.com. $$$$

Texas

In the Lone Star State, barbecue is gospel. Nowhere is this more apparent than in Texas Hill Country, a land inhabited by spirited pit masters that runs from the suburbs of San Antonio to the neighborhoods of downtown Austin. It's a place that has inspired a generation of road-trippers searching for smoky ribs, fork-tender brisket, and sausages charred to perfection. Read on for a finger-licking tour de force.

Cooper's Old Time Pit Bar-B-Que

What was once a remote stopover in the tiny town of Llano has become a hallowed barbecue mecca thanks to the fire-stoking prowess of hometown boy Terry Wootan. The no-fuss restaurant's claim to fame: a two-inch-thick pork chop slathered with a spicy sauce that's available to go. You may just find George W. Bush hunched over a plate of pork ribs on your way out. *604 W. Young St., Llano; 325/247-5713; coopersbbqllano.com.* $$

Franklin Barbecue

How does a youthful newcomer shake up an establishment that wears its loyalty on its sleeve and is run by a none-too-secret society of grillers? Ask Aaron Franklin, who opened a food truck in a nondescript parking lot in East Austin in 2009 and watched it take off. The trailblazer now feeds legions of 'cue worshippers at a wildly successful brick-and-mortar location, where the lines begin before 9 a.m. (the smoked turkey and brisket sell out every day around 2 p.m.). Equally deserving of all the hype is the massive "tipsy Texan" sandwich, made with juicy chopped beef and sausage. *900 E. 11th St., Austin; 512/653-1187; franklinbarbecue.com.* $$

Louie Mueller Barbecue

The first thing you notice at this James Beard Award–winning chophouse: its sooty black walls, the result of 64 years spent smoking meat. None of the patrons seem to mind, though, because pit master Bobby Mueller (son of Louie) cooks up the sort of dishes carnivores crave, from salt-and-pepper brisket sizzled in the restaurant's 54-year-old brick pits to the enormous "dino ribs." *206 W. Second St., Taylor; 512/352-6206; louiemuellerbarbecue.com.* $$

Maywald's Sisterdale Smokehouse

Patrons wait literally weeks for the oak-smoked offerings at this spot just south of Luckenbach—it's open only every other weekend. But the crisp chicken and tender cuts of sugar-and-spice-rubbed beef, prepared in an old trailer using a classic 1973 Oyler pit and served in a renovated barn, are well worth it. *1123 FM 1376, Sisterdale; 830/324-6858; sisterdalesmokehouse.com.* $$

Milt's Pit BBQ

Slow cooking is a way of life at this ramshackle joint near I-35. Here, the brisket takes on a midnight-black crust, and the jalapeño sausage has a zesty kick that'll have you reaching for your lemonade with each bite. Owners Milt Thurlkill and Bunnie Walling don't bottle the secret sauce, but they'll certainly squeeze some into a makeshift container for you to take away. *208 W. Center St., Kyle; 512/268-4734; miltspitbbq.com.* $

Opie's BBQ

The famous sweet-and-spicy baby back ribs at Opie's, Todd and Kristin Ashmore's metal-shed roadhouse off Highway 71, require more than a few paper towels. The same is true for the decadent side dishes, including a cheesy Tater Tot casserole. And if—after all that—you still have room for dessert, opt for the blackberry cobbler, served warm and topped with a scoop of vanilla. *9504 E. Texas Hwy. 71, Spicewood; 830/693-8660; opiesbarbecue.com.* $$

Salt Lick Bar-B-Que

The Salt Lick isn't your average barbecue operation. Set on a 540-acre ranch complete with oak-shaded patios, a stone-and-wood main house, and vineyard-terraced hillsides, the restaurant is known for its pecan-smoked brisket and beef ribs doused in habanero sauce—recipes that date back to the 19th century and pay homage to the Roberts clan's Mississippi roots. *18300 FM 1826, Driftwood; 512/858-4959; saltlickbbq.com.* $$

Stiles Switch BBQ & Brew

Housed in a 1950's Art Deco–style shopping center in the Brentwood neighborhood of Austin, Stiles Switch—helmed by Lance Kirkpatrick, a protégé of Bobby Mueller—serves up flawless garlic-and-cayenne pork links and creamy banana pudding that's as authentic as it gets. Wash it all down with a pint of Big Bark amber ale, a local craft beer. *6610 N. Lamar Blvd., Austin; 512/380-9199; stilesswitchbbq.com.* $

Pit master Aaron Franklin stoking the fires at Franklin Barbecue. Left: The restaurant's "tipsy Texan" sandwich.

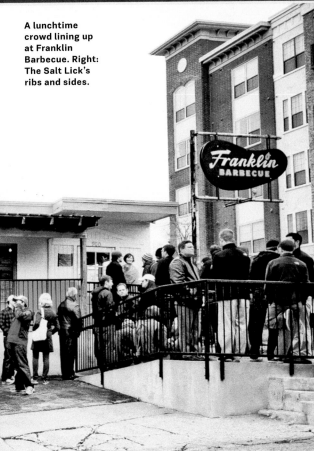

A lunchtime crowd lining up at Franklin Barbecue. Right: The Salt Lick's ribs and sides.

San Francisco, Farm-to-Table

BY ADAM SACHS / PHOTOGRAPHED BY ALEX FARNUM

Dolores Park, in
San Francisco's
Mission
neighborhood.

Bar Tartine's chilled apricot soup and a trio of open-faced sandwiches.

Benu's executive chef, Corey Lee *(left),* and chef de cuisine, Brandon Rodgers. Left: Anchovy, aioli, and sorrel-topped flatbread at Rich Table.

An Asian pear and crème fraîche dessert at Benu. Right: Outerlands's outdoor seating.

had Robertson is the Wheat Whisperer. The earnestly obsessive surfer dude, widely regarded as one of the best bakers in the country, knows stuff about bread that others just don't. Like how to make boring old flour sound interesting. "Kamut is an ancient durum, golden, sweet, and super high in protein," he says of the antediluvian origins of some bread he wants me to try at his rebooted restaurant, Bar Tartine. We're talking about a piece of toast but, as usual when talking with Robertson, I feel as if I'm being inducted into some beautiful, bountiful California dream where everything tastes better and we're all going to live forever. "It's much easier to digest than modern wheats. And it's just so *delicious*."

Robertson and his wife, the pastry chef Elizabeth Prueitt, are known for delicious. The couple opened Tartine Bakery nearby at Guerrero and 18th a decade ago and there's been a line out the door at all hours ever since. San Franciscans should brace themselves for an Occupy-style street protest if the duo were ever to mess with their stable of legendary baked goods. (I will be at the front of the mob, looting trays of gooey, buttery, irreplaceable morning buns.)

Bar Tartine is a different story. Robertson sees the restaurant, which opened a few years after the bakery, as less a static San Francisco institution and more an evolving theater for showcasing the creativity of his staff, visiting chefs, and his own restless enthusiasms. In 2011, he brought in chef Nicolaus Balla—born in Michigan, schooled in Budapest, trained in Japan—and together they changed everything about the place but the name. Then they expanded, adding shiny, Italian-built bread ovens and a lunch business based on Danish smørrebrød (open-faced sandwiches) and puffy Hungarian fried flatbreads called *lángos*.

"It's all a little uncategorizable," Robertson says of the collaboration between baker and chef. "When people ask me what kind of food we're doing, I say, 'Can I write an essay?'"

I'd read it. Especially for the excitable Robertsonian digressions: "We serve a beer from Oakland that's brewed from our bread starter, then the spent grain is brought here and we use it to make Japanese-style pickles...."

Balla once created a menu around the affinity (as he pictured it) between the cuisines of northern Scandinavia and northern Japan—Lapland meets Hokkaido on Valencia Street. The night after I visited, the crew was planning to tackle a nine-course Vietnamese feast. The thing is, right now, in San Francisco, it is utterly conventional for a restaurant with a bustling Danish-Hungarian lunch trade to reinvent itself as Vietnamese for a night.

What's persuasive about the Bar Tartine approach isn't merely a menu that keeps you guessing, that resists easy classification. All this eclecticism comes down to one central tenet (so often, so maddeningly forgotten by chefs tripped up by misguided notions of novelty): it's gotta be, like that mythical, magic Kamut, just *delicious*.

About that toast. It's grilled to a chewy crunch, adorned with golden petals of *bottarga* (cured by Balla from the roe of fish caught by an uncle in Florida) and thrown into umami overdrive by an intense butter flavored with pulverized powders of dried mushrooms and dulse seaweed. What is it? I don't really know. How does it taste? Deeply, saltily, happy-makingly good.

Bar Tartine is, in conception and execution, conspicuously sui generis. But it's also typical—in its funkily atypical way—of a new breed of genre-busting restaurant spreading through the Mission District and reinvigorating the San Francisco dining landscape. The Bay Area is, for anyone who cares about the pleasures of the table, hallowed and fertile ground, cradle of a local-seasonal movement that, however tired we become of hearing those words, really did help change the way a whole country eats.

But in recent years, San Francisco's restaurants have also been, if we're being honest here, kind of a boring scene. Not bad, but predictable, tepid. A few too many chefs swearing too much fealty to the Alice Waters gospel of do-no-harm California cooking. A Groundhog Day of conscientiously curated salads and competent pizzas.

Walk in any direction on Valencia Street these days and it's clear something has come unglued. The

I feel as if I'm being inducted into some bountiful California dream where everything tastes better and we're all going to live forever.

post-puritanical phase of San Francisco restaurants has happily arrived. And it is marked by a loosening of strictures, an increased improvisational eagerness to defy expectations, and a renewed license to get a little weird.

At Abbot's Cellar, a beer-focused restaurant with a mesmerizing wall display of glasses of every imaginable shape and size and an equally expansive menu of draft and bottled brews to fill them, you can pair black lager with your grilled bison loin. Sharing the same building—a high-ceilinged brick structure that was until recently an auto-body shop—is Dandelion Chocolate, a "bean-to-bar" factory and shop, as well as Craftsman & Wolves, an haute patisserie.

Craftsman & Wolves is about as far away, spiritually and aesthetically, from Tartine Bakery (and other folksy Mission sweets spots like Bi-Rite Creamery) as you can get while still occupying the same zip code. My friend Dennis Leary, who owns San Francisco restaurants

Canteen, the Sentinel, and the revamped old-man bar House of Shields, dismisses this new breed as "those ampersand places." But Craftsman & Wolves distinguishes itself from the pack by its Scandinavianesque design and the refined, unapologetically uppity pastries, savory and sweet, tidily arranged, jewel-like, in glass cases. Tacked up on a wall are inspirational quotes from chefs, writers, and architects. One, from Swedish chef Magnus Nilsson, instructs: RESPECT. CONTROL. SELECTION. CONCENTRATION. PRESENTATION.

The sign might as well read LISTEN UP, HIPPIES, THIS IS NOT A CUPCAKE SHOP!

What cuts through the cold is the personality of pastry chef/owner William Werner, which shines in the product itself. The croissants glazed with passion fruit and sesame seeds; a finger of semolina cake studded with candied corn nuts; a very good brownie sandwiched solidly together with caramel; a chocolate-toffee confection that conceals a foie gras *torchon* (or it did until California's idiotic foie gras ban outlawed it in the summer of 2012).

I ate my bagful of pastries first and returned to the counter to round things out with a bit of savory lunch. A jar of pork rillettes was incongruously paired with corn madeleines and two shades of pickled cauliflower. The rillettes were a bit too cold and the madeleines too crumbly, but all the elements stood on their own, and as I sat crunching on Day-Glo purple and yellow cauliflower florets and nibbling potted pork off the tip of a knife, I found myself thinking for the hundredth time since I got to town: here is something I wouldn't be eating anywhere else.

The Mission is the kind of place that can sustain two varieties of street accordionist. There is the hipster accordionist, stationed across from Freemans Sporting Club, wearing a tiny fedora and a beatific smile. And there is the older, wandering, cowboy-hatted Mexican accordionist, looking as though he's not quite sure what's happened to his neighborhood. These blocks have always been a destination for some of the city's best old-school, no-frills taquerias, but what wasn't here until recently was a brightly tiled, sceney spot like Tacolicious (and Mosto, its tequila-bar annex), where you can get pitchers of margaritas made with

Park Tavern's smoked-salmon toast. Below: Sharing a bite outside Wise Sons Delicatessen.

blackberry and tarragon and perfect little tacos of succulent prickly pear and melted *queso oaxaca*.

'd describe the San Francisco restaurant scene as more 'warm and fuzzy' than 'center of the universe,'" says David Lynch, every wine nerd's favorite sommelier and an East Coast émigré. The onetime Babbo general manager left New York to work at sibling Italian restaurants Quince and Cotogna before striking out on his own at St. Vincent, his tavern on Valencia near 24th Street.

The joint is named for Saint Vincent of Saragossa, patron saint of wine- and vinegar-makers, but it's the fuzzy-faced grump Lynch who looks after the thirsty and hungry here—and their needs are well met. Want to start with some grower champagne, head into a cult white from Lazio, and end the night with some funky Catalan red (all for less than a $100 a bottle)? Lynch can take you there. Feel like a pork-rib riff on Kentucky burgoo or a bar snack of beet-purple pickled egg that tastes like a bite of horseradishy borscht? Chef Bill Niles's Southern-inflected, nonconformist menu has your moods covered.

"Sometimes I do miss the edge of New York, but honestly I can't imagine being anywhere else," Lynch says. "We can be a little self-righteous about it, but the fact is San Francisco is just a fount of good shit right now. What we lack in coolness we make up for in kindness."

And the city continues to atone for its fallow period of culinary dullness by fostering niche outlets to meet every curious craving, even the ones you didn't know you had. The Mission in particular feels like it's been laid out by some kind of WPA agency established to stamp out the munchies. Feel like more pickled eggs? Try Pig & Pie, artisanal sausage makers working out of an old record store (the neon marquee still reads DISCOLANDIA). To get there, leave St. Vincent and walk east down the hill on 24th. Cross Mission Street to the shady side and stay on 24th past the vendor selling Mexican wrestling masks, past the "fresh Kombucha bar," past Philz Coffee, where the Palestinian owner grinds beans fresh for every cup, and past the tour groups gathered around murals of Aztec gods and giant flowers. Carry on by the Salvadoran *pupusería* and the Nicaraguan café and the Chinese doughnut shop and the other Chinese doughnut shop,

The afternoon
scene at
Outerlands, in
Ocean Beach.

past the clothing boutique advertising $2 mini golf and past Humphry Slocombe, where the line snakes out the door for scoops of its "secret breakfast" ice cream (spiked with bourbon and cornflakes). Take a *matzoh brei* breather at Wise Sons Delicatessen, a post-ironic Jewish deli where they brine their own pastrami and the walls are papered with fading Yiddish newsprint. In large type over the door as you exit back onto 24th Street there's a motto that reads like a promise: IN AMERICA YOU CAN EAT CHALLAH EVERYDAY.

Did you see Alice Waters buying tomatoes?" Saturday morning at the farmers' market behind the Ferry Building. The entire city has turned up as usual. Everyone is wondering if everyone else just witnessed the affirming spectacle of Alice Waters buying tomatoes.

I'm distractedly eating cheeseburgers for breakfast with Daniel Patterson, chef and owner of the Michelin-two-starred restaurant Coi. Patterson is a thoughtful guy, known for the cerebral naturalism of his food. Maybe it's better that we missed Waters, as Patterson is also known for an essay he wrote in the *New York Times* entitled "To the Moon, Alice?" In it, he challenged his colleagues in Bay Area kitchens to be more original and chided them for relying too heavily on a "dogma" of sustainable ingredients and menus that amounted to little more than "comfortable home cooking with no particular point of view." Though he expressed his abiding simpatico admiration for Waters and the rightness of her mission, Patterson's plea struck many as an affront and, nearly a decade later, the story still rankles. David Chang, of the Momofuku mini-empire, waded into the same waters with more epigrammatic bluntness: "F—kin' every restaurant in San Francisco is just serving figs on a plate. *Do* something with your food." It didn't really matter that Chang was mostly joking and his quote was taken out of context. The result was predictable. Hurt feelings, recriminations, strained East Coast–West Coast relations. If the food world were international diplomacy, ambassadors would have been recalled. If it were hip-hop, there'd have been a brawl at the Beard Awards.

"It's funny, but this is a very conservative city," Patterson says. "Things have loosened up, and there's a new energy here that's exciting. Customers are open to a greater variety of experiences."

After our cheeseburgers at the 4505 Meats stall, I move on to a post-breakfast snack of their cereal bar with *chicharrones*—basically a Rice Krispies treat crammed with fried pork skin. A great sunny blueness breaks through the dishwater-gray sky. We drink a lot of Blue Bottle coffee. Patterson's kids eat a crate's worth of beautiful Yerena Farms berries and are now darting through the dense forest of adult legs.

"The cooking is mutating now and there's this spirit of experimentation and openness I haven't seen here before," Patterson says. "People are playing around more. They're taking risks, making very personal food. We're even exporting to New York now!" he says, a nod to local hero Danny Bowien, whose Mission Chinese Food recently opened an outpost on the Lower East Side.

He doesn't sound vindicated. Just pleased things turned out this way and eager for a night off to see what this new wave of restaurateurs (many of them former Coi employees) is getting up to.

San Francisco is a constellation of unlike parts, microclimates of sun and fog and hill and valley, held together by a mutual preoccupation with where to park and what's for lunch. Any attempt to complete a survey of the city's latest openings is as famously futile as repainting that big bridge—as soon as you're done, you have to start again.

One afternoon I boarded an outbound Muni tram at the Embarcadero and rode it west until it reached the misty dunes of Ocean Beach. High-rise condos disappeared, replaced by low stucco houses in 1970's-leisure-suit shades of tan and teal. A few blocks from the Pacific, across the street from a shuttered service station and down the road from a tattoo shop with a window display of a plump sea lion wearing a fisherman's sweater, there's an unassuming restaurant-café called Outerlands. The walls are hung with gray-brown planks of weathered wood, plants dangle from nautical ropes, and at lunch there's a little menu of simple good things: a sandwich of ripe tomatoes and roasted eggplant; melted cheese with two runny eggs on top; a bourbon-laced apple cider to guard against the sea-breeze chill of a summer afternoon.

A brunch feast
at North Beach's
Park Tavern.

Brett Cooper, the chef, arrived here via the more rarefied kitchens of Coi and Saison. The restaurant's website is full of the kind of twee twaddle that makes you want to lay your head on the Muni tracks ("Outerlands is a gathering place for sea goers who seek warmth, shelter, food, and fellowship.") But then you go and that California thing happens. The vibe is indeed homey, the organic *levain* bread is delicious, and you sort of do want to stay all day.

In another part of town—it could be another planet, really—Anna Weinberg runs Park Tavern, at the edge of North Beach's Washington Square Park. Petite and peculiar may be the order of the day, but San Francisco is comfortable with success, too, and right now this large, handsome brasserie with its coffered ceiling, slate-gray tiles, and tufted black banquettes is the place to celebrate it. Tech money comes out to play, the girls put on their nice shoes, and everybody looks good in the low, golden light of the bar. Michael Bauer, the *Chronicle*'s long-serving restaurant critic, has likened the place to Jeremiah Tower's legendary Stars. Which is to say, it's the scene everyone wants to be a part of and the food is actually good. Anna's a friend, too, so maybe I'm biased. But the week I'm in town *San Francisco* magazine names her Restaurateur of the Year and, judging by the packed house both times I visit, it seems people agree. Jennifer Puccio's expansive menu of intelligent comfort food soothes many moods: a standout burger; schnitzel with bacon-fat eggs and marinated anchovies; for brunch, a hangover-helper cocktail of Fernet Branca, ginger beer, and lemon (available by the pitcher, should you require it). "My inspiration is always food I want to eat on my day off," Puccio says.

Pleasure, says Bauer, is the dominant theme in San Francisco dining. "That's been true since the gold rush, when there was a house of prostitution on every street and they distinguished themselves by their free lunches. The best lunches got the most men."

What distinguishes menus around town these days, he says, is "how personal they've become. You can look at a plate and know who produced it."

One of the chefs Bauer mentions in this context is Corey Lee, who worked for Thomas Keller for many years before opening his own place in the SoMa district. At Benu, Lee applies the French Laundry–style precision and restraint he internalized as chef de cuisine there to ingredients and dishes that reflect not only his Asian heritage but also his own particular obsessions. The $180, 18-course tasting menu at Benu has moments of real beauty. A bowl of wild-salmon roe with puffed buckwheat conjures taste memories of cold soba. There is Lee's take on a *xiao long bao,* flavored with lobster meat and coral, lobster consommé, and tarragon. Not traditional but better than any soup dumpling I've had in Shanghai. "Every day I spend two hours making those," Lee tells me later, laughing. "I'm enslaved by them. It involves a lot of modern techniques like whisking clarified butter over liquid nitrogen, but the idea is for none of that to show up for the diner." I ask him about one of the courses— eel wrapped in *brik* pastry—and he tells me a long backstory involving Christofle cigar holders, Korean bar snacks, and Thomas Keller's fiancée. "She's very picky. She doesn't eat all sorts of stuff, including Thomas's signature salmon cone that everyone starts with at French Laundry. She just didn't like it."

GUIDE

EAT
Abbot's Cellar
742 Valencia St.; 415/626-8700; abbotscellar.com. **$$$**

Bar Tartine
561 Valencia St.; 415/487-1600; bartartine.com. **$$**

Benu
22 Hawthorne St.; 415/685-4860; benusf.com. **$$$$**

Coi
373 Broadway; 415/393-9000; coirestaurant.com. **$$**

Craftsman & Wolves
746 Valencia St.; 415/913-7713; craftsman-wolves.com. **$$**

4505 Meats
1 Ferry Building; 415/255-3094; 4505meats.com.

Outerlands
4001 Judah St.; 415/661-6140; outerlandssf.com. **$$**

Park Tavern
1652 Stockton St.; 415/989-7300; parktavernsf.com. **$$$**

Pig & Pie
2962 24th St.; 415/401-8770; pigandpiesf.com. **$$**

Rich Table
199 Gough St.; 415/355-9085; richtablesf.com. **$$$**

State Bird Provisions
1529 Fillmore St.; 415/795-1272; statebirdsf.com. **$$**

St. Vincent
1270 Valencia St.; 415/285-1200; stvincentsf.com. **$$**

Tacolicious
741 Valencia St.; 415/285-1200; tacolicioussf.com. **$$**

Wise Sons Delicatessen
3150 24th St.; 415/787-3354; wisesonsdeli.com; no dinner. **$$**

The Golden Gate Bridge. Right: Pouring a fresh cup at Outerlands.

So Lee improvised a replacement, a *tuile* served in a cigar holder with powdered olives as ash and.... Well, somehow this led, years later, to this very nice, crunchy, rich little bite of braised Japanese eel.

Of course, inspired flights of fancy sometimes crash and burn. There's a loony restaurant on Fillmore called State Bird Provisions that has garnered feverishly good notices for its dim-sum-cart-style service scheme and gleefully whackadoodle flavor mash-ups ("pickles, smoked-albacore-lardo butter"; "local boquerones, yeasted sesame pancake, crème fraîche"). I can't explain the appeal of the place any more than I can explain to my mouth why I put that smoked albacore-lardo butter in it. The room is dispiritingly ugly, the stuff I tried tasted muddled to middling, the concept bafflingly misguided. This isn't a case of the emperor's new clothes, more the court jester's new clown shoes.

Let us turn instead to a dish that sounded utterly unpromising on paper but turned out to be one of the nicest things I ate in San Francisco. The chicken-liver mousse with pole beans and dill, topped with a crumbly cracker of *pain de mie*, at Rich Table, an otherwise sane-seeming restaurant in Hayes Valley. The light, salty-sweet mousse bound the beans together; the crunch of the cracker added texture—incongruously, it all worked.

"It's really a riff on the green-bean casserole I had as a kid," said Evan Rich, who owns the place with his wife, Sarah. "The beans are the star of the dish. The cracker on top was a replacement for the fried onions."

With its planked walls and industrial sconces, Rich Table has a certain familiar urban-woodsy aesthetic. But like that liver-beans dish, it works because it's smartly put together.

Rich, another East Coast convert, moved to San Francisco with his wife from New York in 2007. "I hate to say it, but at the time the restaurant scene seemed very one-note," he says. He worked at Coi for a while and remembers Patterson telling him, "The difference between New York and San Francisco is that if you serve an amazing lamb dish in New York, the diner will ask, 'How did you cook that lamb?' And if you serve the same amazing dish here, the diner will ask, 'Where did you get the lamb?' These days, though, chefs here are really working to elevate what they do beyond just putting beautiful product on a plate. They've become bolder."

Nobody's abandoned the local-seasonal-sustainable mantra. They've just stopped repeating it out loud. San Francisco has always been an eater's earthly paradise of the finest produce and fiercest pieties. Now it's developed a personality to match. ✦

Los Angeles

Its countless immigrant enclaves make L.A. the quintessential American city, not to mention one of the most diverse places in the nation to eat. Many of today's food trends took root here, starting with the citywide embrace of all things foreign (Salvadoran *pupusas*; Peruvian ceviche; Vietnamese *pho*; kimchi everything). Now the rest of the country is finally catching on to what Angelenos have known for years: the best ethnic cuisine is often right in your own backyard.

A-Frame
Roy Choi—of Kogi food-truck fame—opened this lively ski-chalet-style restaurant in a former IHOP, but his inventive Korean/Filipino-inflected dishes hint at loftier ambitions (beer-marinated crispy chicken with kimchi and two salsas). For dessert? Cinnamon-pound-cake churros with malted milk and vanilla ice cream.
12565 Washington Blvd.; 310/398-7700; aframela.com. $$

Atlacatl
No-frills restaurant Atlacatl, off Beverly Boulevard, is *the* place to sample the Salvadoran *pupusa*: a mouthwatering disk of griddled corn flatbread filled with tangy-sweet *quesillo* (soft, unripened cow's-milk cheese) and your choice of ground pork, refried beans, squash, or *loroco*, a flower that resembles an asparagus tip.
301 N. Berendo St.; 323/663-1404. $

Ink
Top Chef winner Michael Voltaggio takes an artistic approach to global cooking, joining fresh-caught Dungeness crab and surf clams with spring peas and almonds. A penchant for molecular gastronomy doesn't distract from comforting triumphs such as egg-yolk gnocchi with mushroom brown butter.
8360 Melrose Ave.; 323/651-5866; mvink.com. $$$

Jitlada
The mind-bendingly spicy cuisine of southern Thailand is at the heart of the epic 130-plus-item menu at Jitlada, a cozy Thai Town canteen famed for its fiery *khua kling* (a turmeric-charged dry curry with beef or diced pork). Relief comes in the form of *khao yam,* a cooling salad of rice, lemongrass, Kaffir lime, green beans, and sour mango.
5233 Sunset Blvd.; 323/667-9809; jitladala.com. $$

Lotería Grill
The original Lotería stand is a landmark at the Third Street Farmers' Market; the Lotería Grill serves the same note-perfect tacos in a sit-down setting at four locations scattered across L.A. You'll want to try the *cochinita pibil* (marinated pork, slow-roasted in a banana leaf) and, if available, two of the phenomenal *lengua de res* (tender shredded beef tongue in tomatillo sauce), chased with a *michelada* or a bottle of Mexican Coke—made with real cane sugar, not corn syrup.
6627 Hollywood Blvd.; 323/465-2500; loteriagrill.com. $$

Pho Café
Hard-core Vietnamese-food devotees get their fix at Pho Café, hidden in a derelict mini-mall. The long, narrow room is jammed from noon to night with Silver Lake and Echo Park hipsters nursing outsize bowls of Vietnam's beloved noodle soup. Our favorite: the *pho tai gan,* with toothsome beef tendon and ribbons of raw sirloin that slowly cook in the clove- and cinnamon-spiced broth.
2841 Sunset Blvd.; 213/413-0888. $$

Picca
Perched atop an Italian joint in a New York–style town house, Picca is run by Ricardo Zarate, a sushi chef who draws on his Peruvian roots and the region's tangy *ají amarillo* pepper in such small plates as pumpkin-and-quinoa stew, succulent beef-heart *anticuchos* (skewers), and yellowtail *causas* (mashed-potato morsels topped with fish salad)—a far cry from the Neapolitan pizzas served downstairs.
9575 W. Pico Blvd.; 310/277-0133; piccaperu.com. $$

Shamshiri Grill
With restaurants like Shamshiri Grill, it's no wonder L.A. is nicknamed Tehrangeles. Stylish diners bond over Iranian staples like piping-hot lavash bread and savory *gheymeh bademjan* (eggplant stew). Throw in some Farsi gossip and a melancholy ballad by Googosh (the Persian Barbra Streisand) and you have a meal any homesick exile would savor.
1712 Westwood Blvd.; 310/474-1410; shamshiri.com. $$

Sushi Zo
At Sushi Zo, in sleepy Cheviot Hills, an *omakase* lunch might start with *yuzu-* and spicy-radish-dressed Kumamoto oysters, followed by sea urchin and squid "noodles" formed into perfectly al dente capellini, then end with slices of translucent, ruby-red Hawaiian tuna that glisten like tropical fruit.
9824 National Blvd.; 310/842-3977. $$$$

Picca's crab and yellowtail *causas*. Left: Lunch at A-Frame.

A bartender at Lotería Grill. Left: The restaurant's taco sampler.

LOS FUTBOLIS

Digging in at The Pig & The Lady's stall in the KCC Farmers' Market.

Hawaii's Next Wave

BY PETER JON LINDBERG
PHOTOGRAPHED BY CORAL VON ZUMWALT

Anybody here remember pineapple coulis? Macadamia-crusted mahimahi? Does the phrase "wasabi mashed potatoes" mean anything to you? If you spent any time in Hawaii over the past, oh, 20 years, you may recognize these items from your dinner menu. This story is not about those things. It's been two decades since a coterie of forward-thinking chefs put Hawaii on the culinary map. Seizing on the then-current trend for East/West fusion, they blended classical techniques with Hawaiian ingredients, mixed in bold Asian flavors, and called their style Hawaii Regional Cuisine.

It was a thrilling amalgam, and HRC's star burned brightly for a spell, making celebrity chefs of Alan Wong, Roy Yamaguchi, Sam Choy, and Peter Merriman. But as Pac-Rim fusion's novelty faded, foodies' affections shifted, like those temperamental Kona winds, to more beguiling shores. By the turn of the millennium, the term *fusion* had become a slur.

Which isn't to knock the HRC chefs' chops. Most of the original crew are still doing fine work today— and, for plenty of visitors, their names, dishes, and many restaurants still define Hawaiian food, fickle dining trends be damned.

But something else has happened of late, as a new generation of Hawaiian food pioneers emerges. They've embraced HRC's creative spirit and applied it to more traditional Hawaiian foods, drawing from the islands' past as much as the globalized future. They've amped up their commitment to sustainability, to local farmers and ranchers and fishermen, and to unsung or forgotten ingredients. They've moved past the gimmicky aspects of fusion to embrace its tenets naturally, intuitively, as only pan-ethnic, polyglot Hawaiians could do. They're cooking some extraordinary—often extraordinarily simple—food. And they're making it more accessible, in presentation and price, to Hawaii's workaday population, not just to well-heeled diners and tourists.

That last point is fundamental, and explains a lot about where you'll find the new breed. Hawaii's next wave is cresting not in the fine dining rooms of Waikiki, but in an ever-growing number of roving food trucks, farmers'-market stands, plate-lunch diners, guerrilla pop-ups, surfers' haunts, barbecue pits, and hyper-creative hot dog joints. Suddenly, out of the blue, Hawaii is one of the most exciting places to eat in the country.

The beachhead of the movement is a defiantly casual Honolulu restaurant called Town, run by Oahu-born chef Ed Kenney. With his sleeve tattoos and flair for charcuterie, Kenney would fit right in among the scruffy hipster chefs of Brooklyn, Portland, and Montreal—except he's clean-shaven, built like a surfer, and as Hawaiian as they come. (Kenney's mother, a renowned hula dancer, and father, a Broadway singer and actor, used to headline shows at the Halekulani and Royal Hawaiian hotels from the 1950's through the 70's.)

Flush against the hillsides of suburban Kaimuki, far from the thrum of Waikiki, Town feels more neighborhood canteen than haute-dining mecca. The interior is a study in slacker chic, with hardwood benches, rough-hewn plank walls, and portraits of island farmers hung with easel clips.

The kitchen is far more ambitious. Take that charcuterie: all of it cured in-house, and all made with Hawaiian pork, from the spicy soppressata to the cumin-spiked terrine. Tart pickled star fruit provides the ideal counterpoint.

Kenney's beef comes from the Big Island's Kuahiwi Ranch, where it's pasture-raised and grain-finished for a pleasing minerality balanced with the depth of fat. A seared flatiron steak is served with local watercress and dense, chewy coins of fried *paiai*, or mashed taro root. *Paiai*—the solid form of Hawaii's beloved poi— has all but vanished from island menus, since small-scale production of it virtually ceased and was even illegal for a time. But a native Hawaiian named Daniel Anthony recently began selling his own organic, hand-pounded *paiai*, to the delight of chefs like Kenney. If anything could stand in for fried potatoes with steak, it's this.

Other curious local ingredients find their way onto Kenney's plates. A filet of buttery opah (moonfish) is sprinkled with feathery limu seaweed and sided with *pohole* ferns, lending umami and earthiness to the fish. Town especially dazzles with island-farmed greens and herbs, most of them sourced from MA'O Organic Farms, on Oahu's western shore. I'd always envied Hawaii for its sweet mangoes and apple-bananas, but I never thought I'd envy its ethereal tatsoi, fennel, and kale. Even the bartenders get in on the act, muddling arugula, celery, sage, and fresh turmeric into the cocktails. Indeed, the bar menu is one of Town's high points, especially given the dearth of good cocktails elsewhere. (Most drinks still taste like someone tossed a bag of Starburst into a Vitamix.)

Kenney is one of several island restaurateurs who have traded white linens and wine stems for a more democratic, convivial setting. Henry Adaniya was the toast of Chicago at his acclaimed restaurant, Trio (where wunderkind chef Grant Achatz, now of Alinea, got his start). In 2006 Adaniya shut Trio, left Chicago,

Picking up produce at the KCC Farmers' Market.

KAHUKU LAND FARMS

Salmon with fennel and grapefruit from The Pig & The Lady. Left: Dinnertime at Town restaurant.

and moved to his parents' hometown of Honolulu to start...a hot dog joint. The food at Hank's Haute Dogs is far, far better than it needs to be.

Over on the Big Island, chef Edwin Goto, a veteran of luxury hotel kitchens, downshifted to set up Village Burger, located near a Dairy Queen in a Waimea shopping center. Goto is serious about his farm-to-fork. Not only is the beef local (Hawaii Ranchers red veal; Kahua Ranch Wagyu beef), but so are all the trimmings: Kekela Farms baby greens; Nakano Farms tomatoes; Hawaii Island Goat Dairy chèvre; and Hamakua mushrooms.

Turn up any Saturday at Honolulu's crazy-popular KCC Farmers' Market and you'll be floored by the range of local ingredients on offer: tropical rambutan, sea asparagus, wild mushrooms, bitter melon, abalone, goat cheese, duck eggs, sweet Ewa corn, tangerines, taro, Kona coffee beans, Maui lavender, avocados the size of your head. For a traveler accustomed to islands in, say, the Caribbean—where

fresh local produce is depressingly scarce—the variety and quality of homegrown foods is startling.

"People say we can grow anything in Hawaii, and it's true," says Gary Maunakea-Forth of MA'O Farms. On a tour of the farm's 24 acres, he shows me the new experimental garden, where a blueberry shrub is now thriving in the shade of a papaya tree. (Michelle Obama, who's made multiple visits to MA'O during the First Family's trips to Hawaii, has planted her own small vegetable plot nearby.)

Star fruit, mangosteens, blueberries: Hawaii is blessed with such natural bounty that it's shocking to learn that the state actually imports 80 percent of its food, at a cost of $2 billion a year. Dismaying but true: between the high price of local labor, the loss of farmland to rezoning, and the vagaries of the global supply chain, it's cheaper (at least superficially) for Hawaiians to ship food in rather than grow it themselves. This, in one of the most remote places on earth.

Back on the mainland—and in my own archipelago of New York City—chefs tend to speak of sustainability as an ethic rather than as a necessity. But the locavore argument takes on a very real urgency on a chain of islands 2,500 miles removed from anyplace else.

Of course, before Europeans arrived, the islands' food supply was entirely self-sustaining, thanks to sophisticated farming and fishing systems developed by ancient Hawaiians. "Our ancestors lived here for thousands of years with no imports, feeding a population close to what we have today, by putting every acre of land into production," says Kamuela Enos, of MA'O Farms. "They weren't just dancing hula—they were scientists and naturalists, figuring out how to live on a finite biosystem indefinitely." In the plantation era, however, Hawaiians were steadily driven off their farms and removed from the land. Today, fewer than 1 percent of Hawaii's residents work in agriculture, and fewer still are growing actual food for Hawaiians to eat. (Hawaii is now the world's leading producer of

On Oahu you can eat exceptionally well in the least assuming places.

genetically engineered seed corn—some 10 million pounds of it per year—every ounce of which is shipped overseas, and none of which is even edible to begin with.)

It's no coincidence that the Hawaiian diet has changed drastically as well. Fiber-rich taro was once the islanders' go-to starch; it's been almost entirely replaced by cheap white rice. (Because of blight, taro is challenging to grow, and is priced beyond the reach of many consumers.) Processed, fried, and fast foods have pushed out still more whole foods and fresh produce. In just a few generations, "traditional food" has come to mean gravy-soaked *loco moco* breakfasts, greasy plate lunches (with a double scoop of macaroni salad), and *musubi* rice balls topped with Spam. The state has had an alarmingly high rate of increase in obesity and diabetes, especially among the native Hawaiian population. Poverty plays a huge role in this, of course. There's now a concerted effort among local chefs, farmers, and policy makers to reclaim Hawaii's agrarian roots and to make good food available and affordable across the islands.

Oahu has a reputation for overpriced food, one that's certainly justified at the tonier resorts. But you can also eat exceptionally well in the least assuming places, wearing little more than board shorts and flip-flops. (Trust me, you'll fit in better if you do.)

You can, for instance, find a soul-stirring tuna *poke* made by a Korean lady at the back of the Kahuku Superette, a dingy-looking North Shore grocery store. You can get a fabulous, fiery *pad kee mao* at Opal Thai, a bare-bones surfers' hangout in Haleiwa run by Bangkok-born chef Opel Sirichandhra, who started with a food truck before going brick-and-mortar last November. You could spend a whole afternoon in the food court of Honolulu's Shirokiya department store, sampling hundreds of humble Japanese delicacies— from salmon-roe *donburi* to *yakisoba* (fried noodles), from sautéed okra to hot, gooey, made-to-order *takoyaki* (octopus fritters). You could troll the industrial district near the Honolulu airport to find Mitch's, a hole-in-the-wall fish market that hides one of the city's top sushi bars. You could also make the rounds among Oahu's vaunted food trucks, which have exploded in popularity and number, going from 90 four years ago to more than 250 today. (What, you thought L.A. owned that game?)

Or you could have a great meal at one of the itinerant lunch stands that set up inside local farmers' markets. Best among the current crop: The Pig & The Lady, run by a young Vietnamese-American chef named Andrew Le. His family is there to help: Le's three siblings, plus their Hanoi-born mom and Hue-born dad. (They've also hired a Japanese translator for the bazillion Japanese tourists who descend on the weekend markets.) Le's *bun bo Hue*—the lusty, spicy noodle soup of his father's hometown—is the finest I've had outside Vietnam; if you look serious about it he'll drop in a slow-cooked pig's trotter. The Japanese swoon over *bo la lot* (grilled beef wrapped in betel leaf) and Hoi An–style *com ga* (chicken rice seasoned with turmeric and topped with shredded banana leaf).

Several nights a week, Le takes over one of a rotating array of spaces and sets up a remarkable pop-up restaurant, also called The Pig & The Lady. It's here that the chef really shines, with an ever-changing, five-course tasting menu. A recent dinner started with a knockout punch: Chioggia beets, speck, and raspberries, draped in horseradish crème fraîche and sprinkled with mint. Kaffir lime and Vietnamese lemongrass gave a kick to the salmon cured with Sichuan peppercorns, fennel, and grapefruit. A crispy confit pork belly was plated with pickled onions and black rice purée, topped with a soft quail egg, then drizzled in a *sriracha* vinaigrette.

So hold on a minute. Aren't some of Le's dishes—with their East/West flavor collisions—pretty much what we used to call "fusion"?

Well...yes. We just don't use that word anymore. Yet for many Americans, fusion-by-any-other-name is precisely how we eat now. Young chefs are again turning east (and west, north, and south) for inspiration, and embracing the remix, the hybrid, the mash-up: the Korean taco, the sunchoke-and-beef-cheek shu mai. The "f" word forms the angle at so many zeitgeist-defining restaurants, from Lukshon, Spice Table, and A-Frame in Los Angeles to Mission Chinese, Fatty 'Cue, and Talde in New York. To a new generation of American diners, the once-exotic tastes of lemongrass and kimchi are as familiar as home cooking. These days you'll find a bottle of *sriracha* sauce—the ketchup of the 2010's—on every hipster's table.

What, then, do we call this post-global culinary style? "Transcontinental food"? "Srirachan Cuisine"? Maybe, for once, we should just call it "cooking." For there's a natural, homey quality to the current school. While Reagan-era fusion came off as soulless and inauthentic—like its musical analogue, jazz-rock fusion—today's iteration feels more organic, more real, in part by dispensing with the "authenticity" issue altogether. Chefs have moved beyond both the limitations of tradition and the cloyingness of novelty for novelty's sake. They're aiming not for purity but for pure deliciousness—to hell with where it came from.

Another reason fusion originally lost its cred on the mainland: all those exotic ingredients flew in the face of the emerging locavore movement. In Hawaii that conflict goes out the window. Unlike in, say, Minneapolis—where local *yuzu* and wasabi are nonexistent—Hawaii's brand of fusion cooking runs hand-in-hand with the field-to-fork ethic. If almost anything can indeed be grown in Hawaii, from lychees and persimmons to vanilla and cacao, why

shouldn't island chefs embrace all that bounty, in its myriad combinations?

And so Hawaii, after years out of culinary fashion and favor, finds itself once again in sync with the times, on multiple fronts. But as local chefs are quick to point out, trendiness has nothing to do with it. "This is how Hawaiians have been eating all their lives," says Mark Noguchi, a veteran of top Honolulu kitchens such as Town and Chef Mavro and a leading spokesman for Hawaii's farm-to-table movement. "My entire larder is ingredients I grew up with." So-called fusion cooking—be it refined Hawaii Regional Cuisine or a down-and-dirty teriyaki *loco moco*—never went away here. How could it? From the earliest Marquesan settlers onward, the islands have been defined by far-flung influences, resulting in a remarkable demographic diversity: Polynesian, Filipino, Japanese, Portuguese, Chinese, Malay, British, Vietnamese, and on and on.

"Hawaii has always been a melting pot of ethnicities, cultures, and cuisines, as much as New York or Miami, if not more so," Noguchi says. "Look at us: we *are* fusion. Here it's not just a concept or some fleeting trend—it's a way of life." +

GUIDE

EAT

Hank's Haute Dogs
324 Coral St., Honolulu; 808/532-4265; hankshautedogs.com. $

Kahuku Superette
56-505 Kamehameha Hwy., Kahuku, Oahu; 808/293-9878. $

Mitch's Fish Market & Sushi Bar
524 Ohohia St., Honolulu; 808/837-7774; mitchssushi.com. $$

Opal Thai
66-197C Kamehameha Hwy., Haleiwa, Oahu; 808/381-8091. $$

The Pig & The Lady
See thepigandthelady.com for dates and reservations for the pop-up restaurant. Also visit

their stand at the KCC Farmers' Market (see listing below).

Shirokiya Quality Food Court
Ala Moana Shopping Center, 1450 Ala Moana Blvd., Honolulu. 808/973-9111; shirokiya.com.

Town
3435 Waialae Ave., Honolulu; 808/735-5900; townkaimuki.com. $$$

Village Burger
Parker Ranch Center, 67-1185 Mamalahoa Hwy., Waimea, Big Island; 808/885-7319; villageburgerwaimea.com. $$

SHOP

KCC Farmers' Market
Kapiolani Community College, 4303 Diamond Head Rd., Honolulu; Saturdays, 7:30 a.m.– 11 a.m.

A cup of Hawaii's ubiquitous shave ice. Left: A roadside coconut vendor near Haleiwa.

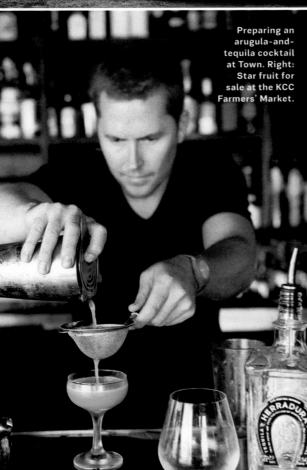

Preparing an arugula-and-tequila cocktail at Town. Right: Star fruit for sale at the KCC Farmers' Market.

The courtyard
of Padrinos,
a restaurant in
Mexico City.

Caribbean + Latin America

Puerto Rico Heats Up

BY PETER J. FRANK / PHOTOGRAPHED BY TARA DONNE

A view of the
beach from
La Concha Resort,
in San Juan.
Opposite:
Longaniza (pork
sausage) and
tostones at
Jose Enrique.

The best meal I have in Puerto Rico is one I shouldn't be eating. I'm sitting at the bar at Jose Enrique, a restaurant near San Juan's lively market square, La Placita, ordering appetizer after appetizer, throwing caution—and my dinner plans—to the wind. After a pair of delicately fried *empanadillas* stuffed with *cetí*, a tiny, translucent river fish, comes a chile-spiked escabeche of black cod, then a plate of thinly sliced octopus with an unexpectedly fragrant Malaysian peanut sauce. The homemade *longaniza* (pork sausage), redolent of garlic and achiote, is paired with salty *tostones*—flattened, twice-fried slices of plantain—that I

splash with the house *pique,* a Day-Glo-orange hot sauce flavored with pineapple and local *ají caballero* peppers, which is as addictive as it is spicy. Just as I think I can't eat another bite, a bowl of luscious braised pork jowls with oyster mushrooms and mashed purple potatoes arrives. By the time the bartender sets down a narrow dish of *tembleque,* the classic coconut pudding in every Puerto Rican grandmother's arsenal (here topped with tiny pearls of cinnamon), I stop glancing at my watch. This is the meal I've traveled all the way to the Caribbean for.

It isn't just the food—at once homey and refined—that has me falling in love with Jose Enrique. Everything about the place reflects Puerto Rico's carefree, tropical vibe. Housed in a small, unmarked Art Deco–like building, it's in the heart of the working-class Santurce neighborhood; as the sun sets, the streets are filling up with people listening to live music and ordering Medalla beers from La Placita's open-air cantinas.

Let other people come to Puerto Rico for its beaches, its rain forest, its dance halls playing salsa and reggaeton. I want to get to know it through my taste buds. And why not? Like Puerto Ricans themselves, the island's cuisine is friendly and approachable, with robust flavors and strong traditions. Eric Ripert, chef of New York City's Le Bernardin, makes annual pilgrimages here to experiment with local ingredients. Ripert devoted an entire section of his book *A Return to Cooking* to the island, calling it "Puerto Rico—A

Spiritual Journey." "Puerto Rican dishes can be humble, but they can also be quite complex," he told me before my trip, pointing to the island's cross-cultural roots (Amerindian, French, Spanish, African) and the lush abundance of tropical produce used in inventive ways. Pork shows up everywhere, whether roasted on a spit or used to enrich *mofongo,* the ubiquitous mound of fried plantains mashed with garlic and cracklings. Pumpkins, yuca, taro, and other starchy tubers are transformed into tamale-like *pasteles,* or they are grated, stuffed with meat, and fried to create an *alcapurria,* a torpedo-shaped fritter that's sold at beachfront kiosks. Passion fruit and mango shine in sauces, cocktails, and desserts. Ripert encouraged me to sample the street food as well as the high-end restaurants, particularly the *alcapurria* shacks in Piñones, right outside San Juan. Which kiosk does he like the most, I asked. "I just head to the least sophisticated one," he said. "That's usually the best."

Driving away from San Juan airport—the jammed highways flanked by big-box stores and fast-food outlets—I am quickly reminded that I'm still in the United States. Ten minutes later, as the road paralleling the runway crosses a bridge and zags right under a canopy of trees, I'm just as fast to forget. Piñones feels like the tropics: cinder-block shacks with corrugated tin roofs and hand-painted signs, a palm-studded beach serving as backdrop. All the kiosks are

The 17th-century Porta Coeli church, in San Germán. Right: A waitress at La Concha Resort.

Grilled swordfish with pigeon-pea escabeche at Pikayo, in San Juan. Left: Wilo Benet, the restaurant's chef.

promisingly dilapidated, so I choose a humble-looking
place with a view of the ocean and a display case full of
deep-fried offerings. I point to a dense-looking mound
that turns out to be a *pionono*—strips of fried ripe
plantains wrapped around a filling of ground beef, then
dipped in an egg batter and fried again. It's sweet and
tasty, but I can't get past the artificial orange hue of the
outer shell. Next I try an *empanadilla* of lobster whose
only reward is a dribble of grease down the front of
my shirt. The quality of the food is supposed to rise in
inverse proportion to the elegance of the venue, but
there's something missing from the equation.

The next day, I point my rental car south to look for
the legendary Ruta del Lechón, which sounds like
something out of a Homer Simpson dream sequence:

a winding mountain road lined with stall after stall
selling *lechón asado*, whole pig roasted on a spit.
This Shangri-la of swine is only a 30-minute drive from
San Juan, in the town of Guavate, where the built-up
suburbs give way to shaggy green mountains. After
a series of dips and switchbacks, I find a half-dozen pig
stands open for business. I stop at the one with the most
cars parked outside and walk up to the counter, where
the pig rests behind glass, a metal spit thrust through its
still-smiling mouth, with skin the color of caramel
and a midsection already partially carved out. I order a
beer and a plate of pork and take them to a picnic table
in an open-air pavilion, the forest stretching out below.
The meat has been cut up into chunks, with some bits
of lacquered skin and gooey pockets of fat. It tastes, well,

piggy, with some traces of garlic and herbs, and a bracing, almost overwhelming tang of salt. This is good *lechón*, but not great *lechón*. I know Puerto Rico can do better.

Alfredo Ayala assures me it can. Ripert had suggested that I look up Ayala, an old friend of his since they cooked together at Joël Robuchon's Jamin in Paris in the 1980's. Ayala is considered a pioneer of modern Puerto Rican cuisine, but his last restaurant, Delirio, closed in the spring of 2010, a victim of the recession. Now he is working as a consultant at the Copamarina, a low-key beach resort in Guánica, a 30-minute drive from the southern city of Ponce. He's a reserved man who worries about the island's culinary heritage. "You can't get good *lechón* in Guavate anymore," he declares at least once, when not lamenting the demise

Let other people come to Puerto Rico for its beaches, rain forest, and dance halls. I want to get to know it through my taste buds.

of a properly made *mofongo*. Ayala abhors shortcuts and cheap substitutions (at a Ponce restaurant, he winces in embarrassment when I ask for *pique* and a bottle of Tabasco shows up instead). At the Copamarina's restaurant, he serves me a multicourse lunch of typical Puerto Rican dishes: a small, delicate *mofongo* in a fish broth swirled with *pique*; seared local snapper with a stew of small white beans, chorizo, and pumpkin; a refreshing salad with avocado and slices of orange and grapefruit. Dessert is a quartet of ice creams—coconut, ginger, soursop, coffee—made with local ingredients. (The soursop, *guanábana* in Spanish, is my favorite: like the tart love child of a pineapple and a strawberry.) The meal isn't humble, nor is it overcomplicated. It proves Ayala's contention that traditional Puerto Rican food can use a touch of contemporary finesse.

f you're looking for refinement, you'll find it at the Dorado Beach resort, 30 miles west of town. In the 1960's this was the stomping ground for Ava Gardner, Elizabeth Taylor, and their glamorous ilk, but it went fallow in recent decades. In 2012, it was relaunched by Ritz-Carlton, with a jungly spa that emphasizes indigenous ingredients; a restored 1920's Spanish colonial hacienda (yours for a cool $30,000 per night); and—most notably—a restaurant, Mi Casa, helmed by superstar chef José Andrés. Here, overlooking the Atlantic, you can see what happens when Puerto Rican comfort classics meet high-flying Iberian techniques. *Bacalao* (salt cod) gets tweaked with black garlic and hazelnuts. *Lechón asado* comes with caramelized mango. *Coquito*, the coconut-and-rum drink that fuels many a Puerto Rican party, is deconstructed and spherified, Ferran Adrià-style.

But you don't have to leave town to find elegant cooking. Take the Condado, the beachfront community whose last heyday was in the 1960's but that has experienced a revival in recent years. It's home to hip restaurants and renovated hotels, like the Conrad San Juan Condado Plaza and the Condado Vanderbilt. I check in to La Concha Resort, a set piece of Tropical Modernism that could have been beamed here from Miami Beach, down to the honeycomb-patterned brise-soleil and the all-night party in the lobby. There I meet up with Wilo Benet, perhaps the most admired chef on the island, who moved his formal flagship restaurant, Pikayo, to the Conrad Condado Plaza in 2009. Benet is charming and charismatic, a big man with a shaved head who issues a stream of cheerful social commentary about politics, the economy, and the restaurant business. "This is a small town with a big-city attitude," he says of San Juan, describing Puerto Ricans as having worldly palates but a staunch traditionalist streak. Benet decides to take me back to the stalls in Piñones. The key, he explains, is to find one where you can watch the food being cooked fresh. We pull up to a kiosk called Tropical Heat as the cook is forming *alcapurrias* by hand, shaping them with the deftness of a sushi chef and plunging them into a blackened vat filled with bubbling oil, heated by a wood fire. Seconds later, we're gingerly nibbling at the *alcapurrias*, letting the steam escape before devouring the garlicky crab stuffing. They're hot and crisp and incredibly satisfying, especially washed down with the juice of fresh coconut. This is the ultimate beach food—the Caribbean's answer to a Coney Island hot dog.

Benet is enjoying himself, too—probably because I'm giving him an excuse to cheat on his diet—but he also takes pleasure in pointing out Piñones's flaws: the cheap, probably stolen lumber being used as fuel, nails and all; the fritters languishing under heat lamps. These *alcapurrias* taste good because they were made before our eyes with fresh ingredients, but to me, the whole setup—the soot, the palms, the blaring salsa music—makes them taste even better. At Pikayo, the following night, I miss some of that homeyness. The room is undoubtedly elegant, with enormous paintings by local artist Willie Quetzalcoatl, Lucite stools for the ladies' purses, and white-jacketed waiters. The menu is expensive and alludes to Italy and Japan, though my five-course degustation contains plenty of island touches: foie gras paired with ripe plantain; griddled shrimp with a *guanábana* beurre blanc. Everything is artfully plated and flawlessly cooked. But despite the promise of explosive flavors, Benet's food feels timidly seasoned: Puerto Rican food dressed up and made safe and presentable. That's not what I came here for.

Let's face it: much of Puerto Rican food is based on relatively bland ingredients—pork, rice, tubers. These constitute a blank slate that can reflect a chef's tastes and talents, or his flaws. A *mofongo* can be heavy and dull, or it can be ethereal and richly flavored, as Ayala's is. *Fondas*—humble restaurants serving home-style food—can be revelatory (the savory chicken fricassee I ate at Bebo's Café, in Santurce) or uninspired (my greasy rice with pigeon peas at El Jibarito, in Old San Juan).

The lobby bar scene at La Concha Resort.

Island produce pairs well with international flavors: at Marmalade, a buzzy spot in Old San Juan, the island's familiar white beans show up in a soup with black truffles and pancetta. And I loved the Latin-tinged dim sum—egg rolls stuffed with local *butifarra* sausage— at Budatai, a Latin-Asian fusion restaurant in Condado.

But on its own, in the right hands, and with the judicious use of garlic, cilantro, and hot peppers, Puerto

GUIDE

STAY

Copamarina Beach Resort & Spa
Km 6.5, Rte. 333, Guánica; 787/821-0505; copamarina.com. **$$**

Dorado Beach, a Ritz-Carlton Reserve
100 Dorado Beach Dr., Dorado; 787/626-1100; doradobeachreserve.com. **$$$$$**

La Concha Resort
1077 Avda. Ashford,
Condado, San Juan; 800/228-9290; laconcharesort.com. **$$**

EAT

Bebo's Café
1600 Calle Loiza, Santurce, San Juan; 787/726-1008; beboscafe.com. **$**

Budatai
1056 Avda. Ashford, Condado, San Juan; 787/725-6919; ootwrestaurants.com. **$$**

Jose Enrique
176 Calle Duffaut, Santurce, San Juan; 787/725-3518; joseenriquerestaurant.com. **$$**

Lechonera La Ranchera
Km 6, Rte. 173, en route to Aguas Buenas; 787/790-9988; weekends only. **$$**

Marmalade
317 Calle Fortaleza, Old San Juan; 787/724-3969; marmaladepr.com. **$$$**

Mi Casa
100 Dorado Beach Dr., Dorado; 787/278-7217; doradobeachreserve.com. **$$$$**

Pikayo
Conrad Condado Plaza, 999 Avda. Ashford, Condado, San Juan; 787/721-6194; condadoplaza.com. **$$$**

Piñones kiosks
Rte. 187, just east of Isla Verde, San Juan.

Cheese soufflé with spiced guava sauce at Pikayo. Left: A food kiosk in Piñones.

Rican food can be extraordinary. Besides Jose Enrique, the most memorable meal I have in Puerto Rico is not at a restaurant. One morning, Ayala calls up and invites me to join him for *lechón asado* cooked by his friend Apa. Ripert also mentioned Apa and his *lechón*, which he roasts by the side of the road in an open kitchen in the mountains. (In fact, he's brought Apa to New York to roast pigs for events at Le Bernardin.) On weekend mornings, Puerto Ricans pull up to his place in their cars, pick up their orders of roast pork, rice and beans, and *morcilla* (blood sausage), and bring it back for family feasts. During the holidays, Apa goes through as many as 100 pigs a day.

It takes about 30 minutes to drive out of San Juan through bamboo forest and along twisty mountain roads to find the place, a jumble of chain-link fence and corrugated metal surrounding a cinder-block pit. There's a *lechón*, plumped on a nearby farm, turning on the spit; it's been seasoned with only a pungent rub of salt, garlic, and herbs. Apa's father, Nando, made *lechón* right here the same way for many years, as did Nando's father before him. Apa himself, stout and sweaty, focuses on cooking, but Rafael, his childhood friend and partner,

shows Ayala and me around Lechonera La Ranchera, the restaurant they've opened. We sit down and wait for the food to arrive, then dig in. The pork, cut from the shoulder and ribs, is moist and chewy, slick with fat but not greasy. I can detect the garlic, oregano, and cilantro in the salt rub, and the distinct smoky flavor of charcoal, but above all it tastes rich and porky. The sides are all excellent, too: rice and pigeon peas; yuca *pasteles* wrapped in banana leaf; *gandinga,* a rich stew made of pork innards; and, once I get past the concept, even the spicy *morcilla*. Rafael brings dessert: a plate of fresh farmer's cheese, and jellied guava and sour orange pastes. Even after filling myself up, I keep stabbing my fork into another piece of *lechón*. I can't get enough.

Outside, I thank Apa and Ayala, and Rafael points to his house, poking through the foliage on a high ridge a few miles away. "We're just Puerto Rican *hilly-billies,"* he says with a smile, as he uses a penknife to shave a matchstick into a toothpick. He nods at a tree that supplied the sour oranges. "The guavas come from a tree across the street," he adds. That's why the dessert, and the whole meal, felt so right: it was made at home, just like I'd hoped to find. ✦

Mexico City

Look past the humble taquerias and festive outdoor markets and you'll find a cadre of homegrown chefs pushing Mexico City's food scene to new heights. With trendy spaces offering contemporary updates on traditional recipes—plus a modern focus on mixology—there's never been a better time to discover the city's hottest restaurants.

Azul Histórico

Ricardo Muñoz Zurita creates textbook examples of iconic dishes—as you'd expect from a chef who wrote an encyclopedia on Mexican cuisine. His fourth restaurant is in a laurel-shaded courtyard next to the chic Downtown México hotel where patrons linger after meals sipping mezcal from jicaras (gourd bowls). In addition to an ever-changing roster of à la carte soups, moles, and enchiladas, there are frequent stints by guest chefs and menus devoted to regional specialties. *30 Isabel la Católica; 52-55/5510-1316; azulhistorico.com.* **$$$**

Belmondo

Stylish members of the once rundown Roma neighborhood's creative class line up at this unpretentious café decorated with Midcentury chairs and industrial light fixtures. The menu is straightforward: salads, pitch-perfect sandwiches (try the grilled cheese on brioche with caramelized onions), and a well-edited list of wines by the glass. Need proof of its hipster cred? Members of Radiohead ate here several times during a recent tour. *109 Tabasco; 52-55/6273-2079; belmondoroma.com.mx.* **$**

Contramar

When fashionable locals long for simply prepared seafood, they head to Andrés Barragán's airy spot in Roma. A high-ceilinged, blue-and-white dining room—it could have been airlifted straight from Mykonos—is the setting for loud, convivial lunches, especially on weekends. What to order: chipotle-mayonnaise-topped tuna loin tostadas to start, followed by the *pescado a la talla,* grilled porgy painted with green and red sauces. *200 Durango; 52-55/5514-9217; contramar.com.mx.* **$$$**

Dulce Patria

Fans of Martha Ortiz Chapa's shuttered Aguila y Sol celebrated when the chef resurfaced in 2010 at the glamorous boutique hotel Las Alcobas. The stark-white walls and sharp edges of her 80-seat cantina act as a blank canvas for bold, whimsically presented dishes: multicolored squash-blossom quesadillas with *salsa verde,* roasted pork tenderloin topped with leafy herbs, and orange sorbet with animal crackers. *100 Anatole France; 52-55/3300-3999; dulcepatriamexico.com.* **$$$**

Padrinos

The prize for best use of greenery goes to Padrinos, also near the Downtown México hotel: a patio wall doubles as a vertical garden complete with a bicycle parked upright. Artists and boutique owners dine on a mix of modern *antojitos* (street food), such as *chicharron de atún* (tuna cracklings), and Mediterranean entrées such as saffron-and-truffle risotto. *30 Isabel la Católica; 52-55/5510-2394; bajodelatintorera.com.* **$$**

Pujol

It may have opened in 2000, but Pujol is still the city's most creative showcase for Mexican cuisine. Experimental chef Enrique Olvera uses modern techniques and nothing but the freshest ingredients. Take his version of the classic toasted corn snack *elote,* glazed in a coffee mayonnaise and sprinkled with ant powder (yes, the insect variety). There are tacos, too, filled with baby lamb, avocado-pea purée, and *hoja santa,* an aromatic herb. *254 Francisco Petrarca; 52-55/5545-3507; pujol.com.mx.* **$$$$**

Quintonil

The latest hit in Polanco is a bright, narrow room where Jorge Vallejo, a disciple of Enrique Olvera, serves up dishes that look like floral arrangements and taste unexpectedly delicate. *Huauzontles,* a broccoli-like vegetable, are fried and topped with tomato salsa and a crumbly cheese from Chiapas; curlicues of *chilacayote* squash and charred tortillas are drizzled with house-made mole. Be sure to save room for the mandarin *panna cotta.* *55 Isaac Newton; 52-55/ 5280-2680; quintonil.com.* **$$$**

Romita Comedor

The food is rivaled only by the setting at Romita Comedor, a theatrical, greenhouse-type space with checkerboard floors and a retractable glass roof. You can't go wrong with the *taco del río,* made with langoustines in a tomato-and-morita-chile sauce. At night, the city's cocktail tribe packs the bar for inventive drinks, such as the margarita made with mezcal and passion fruit, or a milky avocado *horchata* martini. *49 Álvaro Obregón; 52-55/5525-8975; romitacomedor.com.* **$$**

Patio dining at Padrinos. Left: Quintonil's chef, Jorge Vallejo.

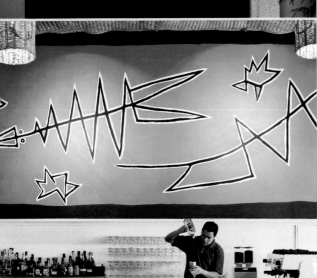

Contramar's raw-tuna tostadas. Left: A fish mural behind the restaurant's bar.

A breakfast of house-made granola and fruit at Belcampo Lodge.

The Wild Heart of Belize

BY SHANE MITCHELL
PHOTOGRAPHED BY TARA DONNE

My first night at Belcampo Lodge is punctuated by what sounds like Ozzy Osbourne being strangled in the pitch-darkness. The cottage is suspended in a dense canopy of hanging vines and gumbo-limbo trees, providing natural privacy, so I've traded my bed for a hammock on the screened porch to feel closer to this forest primeval. A breeze rattles palm fronds as a rain shower sweeps through, carrying the scent of jasmine. Nuts hit the corrugated zinc roof and roll to the ground far below. Suddenly, just before dawn, the Ozzy-like roar of a troop of howler monkeys bolts me upright— and it's resoundingly clear that I'm bivouacking beyond my comfort zone.

Readying Belcampo's terrace for dinner. Left: Fresh tortillas.

By first light, their screeching has faded, giving way to the soft clicks of keel-billed toucans. Soon I'm seated on the lodge's veranda with a pair of binoculars, keeping an eye on the cotton tree where these colorful birds hop from branch to branch, until breakfast arrives: a plate of "fry jacks" (puffy tortillas), sour-orange marmalade, nutty granola sweetened with coconut, and cinnamon-bark-smoked bacon. I could linger long into the morning, watching the toucans play, but I want to see where baby chocolate bars are born.

At the end of a steep driveway lined with torch ginger and flowering trumpet vine, the landscape opens up to a broad valley that the Belcampo farm team has planted with cassava and banana cover crops. Inside the nursery I meet manager Kenny Ramos, a tall, shy man with a passion for vanilla orchids and rare varieties of cacao. In his spare time he hunts for wild plants in untrammeled corners of Belize and tracks their genetic profiles.

Surrounding us are thousands of cacao saplings. Ramos picks one up and points to a pale green bud grafted onto its woody stem.

"Criollo," he says quietly.

"*That's* what you hiked three days into the jungle to find?"

Ramos simply shrugs, implying it was a walk in the park, albeit a park populated with deadly fer-de-lance and coral snakes. I touch the tender criollo shoot carefully. Might this be a direct descendant of the mysterious "white cacao" that the Maya first domesticated 2,500 years ago? The fabled lost bean that Columbus tasted on his fourth voyage to the New World? The holy flavor grail among artisanal confectioners? It is enough to make a chocoholic go weak in the knees.

Belcampo belongs in the vanguard of the next culinary travel trend: more field expedition than farm stay, a full-immersion Belize travel experience for intrepid foragers who want to walk on the wilder side, discovering and tasting exotic edibles on a 1,000-acre plantation and adjacent 12,000-acre wilderness reserve complete with jaguars

A heliconia plant in Belcampo's jungle. Right: Crushing cacao nibs at the farmers' market in Punta Gorda.

and boa constrictors. Originally built as a fishing camp, the property has been reimagined and rebranded to take better advantage of the extraordinary natural resources in the remote Toledo district of southern Belize. Its 12 guest cottages are scattered along a hill that drops abruptly to the banks of the slow-moving Rio Grande, which flows from the Maya Mountains on the Belize-Guatemala border to a mangrove-lined outlet on the Caribbean Sea, just eight miles away as the crocodile swims. From the lodge's hilltop perch, the rain forest unfolds in every direction: a vast green mansion that shelters more than 60 percent of this Central American country.

Guiding Belcampo's ongoing transformation are owner Todd Robinson, a conservation-minded investor from California, and CEO Anya Fernald, a former Slow Food Foundation director. They have embarked on an ambitious "farm of origin" project, proving that the concept of *terroir* doesn't apply just to wine. Fernald has forged relationships with discerning cacao and coffee buyers, including Katrina Markoff of Vosges

Haut-Chocolat and James Freeman of Blue Bottle Coffee. They come to Belcampo to source rarefied ingredients, as well as to share their expertise during culinary excursions and master classes: Markoff has tailored a weeklong "bean to bar" chocolate course, and Freeman does the same for coffee aficionados. (Coffee and cacao are still emerging crops for Belize, compared with Costa Rica, Ecuador, and Venezuela. When Belcampo's criollo trees mature—they're still four years from first harvest—the estate will be the largest single grower of cacao in the country.) Belcampo also plans to produce its own rum, from cane raised on the property. Meanwhile, the estate is swiftly becoming self-sufficient: raising chickens and pigs; growing fruits and herbs in a three-acre kitchen garden; even harvesting rosewood from the surrounding jungle to craft service pieces for the dining room. Belcampo's farm is the source for nearly everything on the menu, from the poached eggs served on boiled *chaya* leaves at breakfast to the mint in the mojito muddled during cocktail hour.

Kayaking on the Rio Grande, which flows through Belcampo.

"*Agritourism* is such a sticky word," says Fernald, who has flown in from California to check on the new education center, where culinary courses are held. "Our guests learn about an ancient, integrated way of growing food in an isolated country off the global trade routes." Under a *palapa* in the kitchen garden, we discuss the appeal of distinct cacao varieties as Ramos cracks open several mature pods to expose raw beans encased in creamy white pulp. One has an astringent citrus note, another is more floral.

Fernald has serious foodie chops, having worked on culinary and agricultural initiatives in more than 30 countries, from cheese making in Sicily to cattle ranching in Uruguay. (She is also a regular judge on *Iron Chef America*.) There's an impressive cookbook collection in the lobby and a shiny new La Marzocco espresso machine in the dining room. To round out the experience, Belcampo's staff will escort guests to nearby cacao and spice farms, as well as a weekly market in the regional capital.

Market days start early in Punta Gorda. Fortunately, the howler monkeys are a fail-safe alarm clock. I ride into town just after sunrise on Saturday, in the company of one of the guides. On Front Street, I join other customers pinching the produce. All around me, vendors are selling provisions unavailable in the outlying villages: fresh seafood, Tupperware, yards of lace, secondhand jeans. Children weave through the crowd hawking frozen bananas dipped in chocolate and toasted coconut. Under the shade of makeshift stalls, Mayan women, wearing gold hoop earrings and ruched blouses, sit next to piles of cassava, turmeric, dried beans, and bottles of homemade habanero sauce, while on the opposite sidewalk, bearded Mennonite farmers, in their straw hats and suspenders, unload juicy watermelons and broccoli. It is the weirdest juxtaposition of agriculture. And of cultures. Belize isn't so much a melting pot as a hotbed of runaways and renegades, where descendants of Confederates, Caribbean slaves, indentured East Indians, British buccaneers, and indigenous Mesoamericans all cling to their own culinary traditions under one shared jungle canopy. I buy a sack of roasted pumpkin seeds from a lady wearing a purple gingham apron, then watch another make hand-kneaded tortillas on a heated metal disk called a comal.

Along Punta Gorda's waterfront, I'm lured by the sweet aroma issuing from Cotton Tree Chocolate. I push open the shop's screen door and get a quick tour of the premises. They do it all here, from roasting beans to molding candies. In traditional Mayan households they use a *ca'aj,* a curved rock mortar, to temper cacao beans, rolling them swiftly back and forth until they're ground to a coarse paste. This pure form of chocolate is diluted with hot water for a strong-flavored beverage that provides a bigger jolt than coffee. The shopkeeper gives me a sample chunk of intensely dark chocolate that melts on my tongue. It's as good as any from Paris or New York confectioners—better, maybe, for being tasted so close to the source.

Belcampo belongs in the vanguard of the next culinary travel trend: more field expedition than farm stay.

Back at the lodge, my next horticulture lesson involves a 27-inch machete. Bumping through a cleared field at the base of Machaca Hill, Kenny Ramos steers a Polaris four-wheeler onto a rutted mud track. We enter a twilight zone of tangled vegetation. Francisco Ack, another of the farmhands, climbs off and sizes up several cohune palms. This is a mother plant: the fronds are used by the Maya for thatch; the nuts produce cooking oil; the inner bark provides food for pigs and chickens. Nothing goes to waste. After a few rasps of the blade on a whetstone, Ack hacks away at the cohune until the core is exposed. Then he hands over the machete. Ramos instructs me to hold it with two hands, like a baseball bat.

Thunk, thunk. Wielding a knife more than two feet long takes more precision than I'd expected, especially when slicing a wedge into what resembles an oversize artichoke. The men whacking at unruly grass in the fields had made it look effortless. I pass the blade back to Ack to finish the job. He chops the palm down and sections out its heart in a matter of minutes.

The creamy-looking center, when cooked, can easily feed two dozen people.

At a family-style dinner at the lodge that evening, the palm heart is prepared two ways: slivered over salad greens and boiled to a pulp with fresh turmeric root until it resembles an East Indian *palak paneer*. Kimchi made from cabbage raised in the garden is served alongside johnnycakes and black-bean dip. Next, fried cassava sticks, which we dunk in salsa spiked with leafy *culantro*, a tropical cousin of coriander. Barbecued chicken glazed with rum and brown sugar and a pork loin simmered in coconut cream are luscious and homey. (The backgrounds of Belcampo's staff range from Maya and East Indian to Garifuna, an ethnic minority from St. Vincent, who are masters of Caribbean-style slow braising.) There's even a ceviche of lionfish, a spiny little invasive that has been rapidly overwhelming local reef species; the flesh is surprisingly delicate and flavorful when filleted and cured with lime.

On my final afternoon, I go out on the river with Emmanuel Chan, one of Belcampo's resident bird experts. He meets me in the lobby, dressed in khaki from head to toe; from here a tram drops us down through the rain forest to a dock on the Rio Grande. Chan launches two kayaks, and we paddle against the lazy current. The banks are thick with blooming swamp iris and jipijapa palms. A heron startles and flies off around the bend.

Chan points to a dark, furry silhouette high in a mahogany tree. "You don't see lone howlers often," he says. "That's probably a juvenile male who's been pushed out of the troop." Chan tries to get the monkey's attention, but it ignores us, asleep in the heat of the day. No doubt the onset of dusk will change that. I'm just glad to finally spot one of these raucous jungle creatures, whose night music has colored my dreams. +

A farm-to-table take on huevos rancheros. Above: The screened porch of room No. 12.

GUIDE

STAY & EAT
Belcampo Lodge
Punta Gorda;
belcampoinc.com. $$$

DO
Cotton Tree Chocolate
2 Front St., Punta Gorda;
cottontreechocolate.com.

Buenos Aires

Eat your way through the colorful barrios of Buenos Aires and one thing becomes abundantly clear: Argentines take their food seriously. While grass-fed beef and wood-fired empanadas still enjoy a vaunted—and much deserved—place, pioneering chefs are steering Porteños toward more multicultural dishes and new-age concepts. Below, a look at the city's best age-old *parrillas* and forward-thinking restaurants.

Cocina Sunae

What could be better than an intimate dinner party thrown at the house of a local chef? At her discreet, reservations-only *puerta cerrada* (or residential supper club), Christina Sunae re-creates Southeast Asian comfort food from her childhood. You may start with the *sinigang*—a Filipino soup made with pork broth, shrimp, and taro root—then move on to the spicy *khao soi*, chicken with egg noodles in a coconut-curry sauce. *Colegiales; cocinasunae.com.* **$$**

El Muelle

For years, only fishermen could access the jetty that juts from the Avenida Costanera into the Río de la Plata. This changed with the opening of El Muelle, a seafood spot on the pier that has quickly won a loyal following with its fresh spider crab and grilled wreckfish salads. *Avda. Costanera Rafael Obligado and Avda. Sarmiento; 54-11/4773-2216; elmuelle restaurante.com.ar.* **$$$**

Experiencia del Fin del Mundo

At the limestone-walled tasting room of Patagonian winery Bodega del Fin del Mundo, flights follow a single varietal through several vintages. Try a range of Malbecs with regional plates such as caper-topped beef carpaccio or Neuquén venison with smoked apples and bacon. *5673 Honduras; 54-11/ 4852-6661; bodegadelfindel mundo.com.* **$$$**

Fervor

Head to this checkered-floor brasserie for an introduction to classic Argentinean cuisine. Order the iconic *asado de tira*—14-inch, crosscut ribs dry-aged for 21 days—or delve into the extensive seafood selection, which includes briny white salmon and skewers of char-grilled baby squid. *1519 Posadas; 54-11/4804-4944; fervorbrasas.com.ar.* **$$$**

La Cabrera

Pretty young things sip champagne on the sidewalk while they wait for tables at La Cabrera, a traditional *parrilla* where waiters in berets deliver cuts of seared beef topped with rosemary and thyme along with meat-friendly sides like mashed squash, Andean potatoes, and broiled onions. *5099 Cabrera; 54-11/4831-7002; parrillalacabrera.com.ar.* **$$**

La Pulpería (El Federal)

At lunchtime, Palermo's in-the-know gastronomes go to La Pulpería, an old-school diner that specializes in offbeat flavor combinations (don't miss the oyster-and-mushroom sandwich) and fresh-baked *alfajores*, sugar-dusted shortbread cookies with jam or creamy *dulce de leche* filling. *1667 Uriarte; 54-11/4833-6039; pulperiaargentina.com.ar.* **$$**

La Vinería de Gualterio Bolívar

In the historic San Telmo neighborhood, the 12-seat La Vinería de Gualterio Bolívar is ground zero for BA's molecular gastronomy movement. On El Bulli–trained chef Alejandro Digilio's 10-course tasting menu: a rustic bone-marrow stew made with collards and *farofa* and a multi-textured vegetable-and-herb salad. *865 Bolívar; 54-11/4361-4709; lavineriadegualteriobolivar.com.* **$$$**

Leopoldo

Bocuse d'Or–winning chef Diego Gera whips up intensely flavored signature dishes such as crisp-skinned suckling pig paired with quince purée at this contemporary space in Palermo. After dinner, the chic crowd migrates to the patio for sour amarena-cherry cocktails. *3732 Avda. Cerviño; 54-11/4805-5576; leopoldo restaurante.com.ar.* **$$$**

Paladar Buenos Aires

In the far-flung Villa Crespo barrio, Paladar is another of the city's most sought-after *puertas cerradas,* thanks to chef Pablo Abramovsky's fresh crispy shrimp rolls and cooked-to-perfection Argentinean salmon. *Acevedo and Camargo; paladarbuenosaires.com.ar.* **$$**

Social Paraíso

Chef-owner Federico Simoes is the driving force behind Social Paraíso. His mission: to shake things up with cutting-edge dishes like Patagonian prawns prepared with tabbouleh salad, spinach, and mushrooms; Sichuan-pepper ice cream; and passion-fruit mousse. *5182 Honduras; 54-11/4831-4556.* **$$**

Christina Sunae in the kitchen of her Cocina Sunae. Left: The bar at Palermo's Leopoldo.

El Muelle's shrimp risotto. Right: Café culture on a Buenos Aires side street.

Savoring São Paulo

BY ANYA VON BREMZEN / PHOTOGRAPHED BY DAVID NICOLAS

Chef Sergio Torres
(center) and
his staff at Eñe
restaurant.

Chef Helena
Rizzo of Maní.
Right: Regional
cachaças
at Mocotó.

The São Paulo
skyline. Left:
Cured *bottarga*
with daikon
and *mitsuba* at
Kinoshita.

ong past midnight at the restaurant D.O.M., in São Paulo, my partner, Barry, and I are sniffing out exotic notes (anise? banana?) in the Anísio Santiago cachaça. Produced in minuscule batches in the colonial state of Minas Gerais, this is the Sassicaia of sugarcane spirits. "The refinement of the best grappa," I suggest, in a daze. "With the brawn of moonshine supreme...," offers Barry. Our travel fatigue (we've just flown in from New York) gives way to a pleasant delirium as we take in the surroundings. Armored SUV's await tanned CEO's at the entrance to this soaring beige space. At the next table, a clutch of French celebrity chefs

(in town for a food event) ogle fantastical blondes in Diesel jeans and Louboutin heels. The blondes in turn glance adoringly at D.O.M.'s chef-owner Alex Atala.

A dish with five striking iterations of okra—sautéed, roasted, fried, reinvented as translucent paper, and turned into a crunchy caviar of its seeds—arrives. I examine my notebook, trying to make sense of flavors and names: fettuccine of pupunha (palm heart). Purple Amazonian basil scattered over a green tomato gelée. Vinaigrette of citronella ("An herb," I've scribbled, "used by jungle natives as insect repellent"). At this late hour an exquisite dish of brioche-breaded oysters, under a glistening heap of lime-marinated tapioca pearls accented with Brazilian soy sauce, here seems less like chef-y artifice than some postmodern, postcolonial inevitability. *Here* being a multicultural, 11-million-strong megalopolis teetering on the brink of the future in a present of helipads, favelas, behemoth traffic jams, and celebrated street art that's both wildly colorful and edgily feral.

Actually, scratch that: the future is already here at D.O.M. and a handful of other São Paulo restaurants whose chefs meld avant-garde European techniques with native ingredients in a distinctly original style. South America's largest city has become the talk of the food world, a required stop for international mega-chefs from Alain Ducasse to Ferran Adrià (not to mention ravenous gastronauts like myself). Subtropical warmth,

high-energy urbanism, and Brazilian sexiness blend to deliver a cuisine that dazzles like no other.

At D.O.M., possibly the world's Next Great Flavor lands on our table. It's a weird root, hairy and scratchy. *"Priprioca,"* Atala says, flashing his charismatic grin. "Amazonian natives use it for cosmetics." After discovering that *priprioca* was edible, Atala has been extracting its essence to use in desserts. Its aroma ("grassy; a suggestion of dope") infused the caramel served with the transparent banana-and-lime ravioli we'd just had. *Priprioca* is Atala's latest obsession— along with every possible by-product of manioc; *turu* (anyone for mangrove worms with a flavor of oysters?); and *jambu* (a tongue-numbing Amazonian green).

Trim-bearded and tattooed, the fortyish Atala looks like a rock-star chef, which he is, and a former punk-rock DJ, which he was before he went backpacking in Europe at the age of 19 and enrolled in catering school in Belgium so he could acquire a work visa. Returning to Brazil in 1994, he opened D.O.M. five years later and today spearheads Brazil's food revolution. Forager, fisherman, environmentalist—and for my money one of this planet's most exciting chefs—Atala is an evangelist, spreading the word about Amazonian foodstuffs around Brazil and beyond. Extreme *terroir*-ism is easy in Europe, it occurs to me after another gulp of cachaça. Another matter altogether is the Amazonian rain forest, home to the world's largest collection of flora and fauna.

"A new pride in Brazilian flavors!" exclaims my friend Luiz Camargo, a local food-magazine editor, over lunch the next day in the chichi Jardins district (where São Paulo resembles Beverly Hills). "It's huge news in this globalized city of immigrants, which used to import foreign chefs and treat them like idols and role models."

Veneration of haute imported chefs notwithstanding, immigrant cultures are what made São Paulo such an exciting food city from the get-go, even before the current explosion of interest in locavore flavors turned it into the world's newest culinary mecca. Founded in 1554 by Portuguese Jesuit missionaries, Sampa (as the locals call it) received a vast influx of immigrants throughout the 19th century—but particularly after the abolition of slavery in 1888, when foreign labor was needed to work the coffee plantations surrounding the city. Italians brought pizzas, Germans brewed their beer, the Japanese transformed farming.

South America's largest city has become a required stop for international mega-chefs and ravenous gastronauts alike.

"So we mix pasta, sushi, *feijoada,* and Portuguese salt-cod fritters," Camargo explains. "It's always been perfectly natural here."

Of course there was Brazilian cuisine, too—itself a hybrid of Portuguese, West African, and indigenous influences. But as Camargo is telling us, until recently, "eating Brazilian" was something relegated to home or to cheap rice-and-beans lunch joints. Barry and I take this all in while still daydreaming about our ur-mid-morning snack: a puffy *pão de queijo* (a round cheese-and-manioc-starch bread) accompanied by a bracing *cafezinho* at Pão de Queijo Haddock Lobo, a tiny takeout counter just down the street.

For a tutorial in contemporary flavors, Camargo has brought us to Dalva e Dito, Atala's more casual restaurant. In contrast to D.O.M.'s flashy experimentation, the adobe-hued Dalva is all about the sharp updating of grandmotherly regional dishes.

Moqueca, a seafood stew from the Afro-Brazilian state of Bahia, normally heavy with its thick film of *dende* (palm oil), tastes clean, vibrant, and coconutty here. To follow: *pirarucu,* a white-fleshed Amazonian fish that can reach 450 pounds. Atala uses the loin of a smaller, more delicate specimen, saucing it with a Brazil-nut vinaigrette. "A typical *caipira* [country folk] meal," Camargo pronounces as the main course arrives. It's *porco na lata,* pork cooked in a tin can into a tender confit. For dessert: silky pastel-hued sorbets in tropical flavors such as *caju* (cashew fruit), guava, and *graviola* (soursop). "Brazil is vast," Camargo says. "Until now, such flavors were as exotic to us Paulistas as they are to you!" He adds slyly: "Alex showed young local chefs that you can be cool *and* Brazilian."

That afternoon we make our way into the fun-house-style museum opening for local heroes Osgemeos, internationally toasted twin-brother graffitists. A band plays a raucous northeastern *forró* beat among the twins' spray-painted fantasies. More *forró* music awaits at lunch at Mocotó the next day. Restaurants don't get any cooler—or more Brazilian—than this cult spot owned by 35-year-old Rodrigo Oliveira, Atala's favorite young chef and disciple. A few years ago Oliveira took over the humble, four-decade-old place from his father—in secret, while Dad was away—tweaking the details but preserving the populist *espírito* and the vernacular flavors of Pernambuco, the northeastern state his family is from. Getting here is an adventure: you ride in a cab for an hour, leaving the city's high-rises and their helipads behind, finally emerging in the ramshackle working-class district of Vila Medeiros. You squeeze onto a bench under the shingled awning outside. Then you wait—and wait—for a table, savoring the block-party vibe with a glass of cachaça. Scouring Brazil's *alambiques* (distilleries) for hyper-artisanal stuff, Oliveira has assembled a list of nearly 350 bottles. Brave them straight or in a rainbow of exotic fruit caipirinhas: milky *graviola,* violet jaboticaba that tastes a bit like tropical blueberry.

When at last we claim a long wooden table inside the color-splashed restaurant decorated with cachaça bottles, the food proves worth waiting for. There's a goat stew in the rustic style of the *sertão* (northeastern backcountry), and the restaurant's eponymous dish, *mocotó,* is a high-octane cow's-hoof soup. Mix it with

Dining at
Eñe. Above: The
restaurant's
oyster-tartare-
stuffed tomatoes.

yellow favas laced with linguica sausage, shredded beef, and cilantro and you get *mocofava*, Oliveira's signature dish. Another standout, *carne do sol* (salted air-dried beef), isn't dry in the least. That's because Oliveira cooks it *sous vide* for 24 hours before serving it smothered with roasted garlic on a hot metal slab. "*Sous vide* cooking of *carne do sol*," Atala says to me later. "This isn't 'molecular gastronomy'—it's a way of advancing Brazilian identity."

Brazil's classic cuisine is, of course, a colonial melting pot of identities. Consider Brazil's answer to cassoulet, *feijoada*—a copious casserole of black beans and various pork parts. "*Feijoada* is a cauldron bubbling with three cultures," someone is saying at our long table at A Figueira Rubaiyat, a Jardins steak house legendary for its Saturday *feijoada* buffet. "The *farofa* (toasted manioc meal) is an indigenous staple; the linguica sausage and collard greens are a Portuguese contribution; many say the whole dish is a creation of African slaves." To this mix Figueira's owners, the Iglesias family, bring a sustainable twist: most of the ingredients come from their *fazenda* (estate) in the fertile southwestern state of Mato Grosso do Sul. Our waiter offers more caipirinhas and a hoary *feijoada* cliché: eat it as slowly and languidly as it was cooked. Four hours later we're still ferrying our plates from the mile-long buffet back to our table under the vast 100-year-old fig tree in the glass-roofed patio. Another helping of creamy *feijao floresta* beans painstakingly simmered over two days; spoonfuls of crunchy *farofa*, emerald ribbons of greens, a few orange segments. Then pig craziness: tender ribs, two kinds of sausages, slow-cooked baby boar, smoked tongue...feet, ears, tail, snout. *Feijoada* is a dish for which the siesta was invented.

To taste the essence of Brazil without the bean-induced slumber, we head to Maní, where the country's national dish has been given a post-molecular treatment by the talented thirtysomething husband-wife chefs Helena Rizzo and Daniel Redondo. A onetime fashion model, Rizzo met Redondo at Celler de Can Roca, the cutting-edge Catalan restaurant where she was an apprentice and he, chef de cuisine. You taste the influence of their mentors, the Michelin-darling Roca brothers, in the Waldorf salad deconstructed into celery ice, apple gelée, and Gorgonzola emulsion, a dish as

Dalva e Dito's *moqueca baiana*, a traditional Brazilian stew with fish, shrimp, and coconut broth.

pretty as a bouquet of spring flowers. Still, the true excitement is in the couple's reinterpretations of Brazilian flavors. For their trompe l'oeil *feijoada*, the intense black-bean liquid is "spherified" into delicate beads (adapting a technique by Ferran Adrià). The black pearls arrive on the plate dotted with bits of linguica and oranges under a crunchy sheath of julienned fried kale. After dinner Rizzo talks about food memories being like "fragments of a puzzle, which over time cohere into a dish that connects us to our roots, amid the endless stimuli and confusion of big cities." I find this thought very poetic, especially in overstimulating São Paulo.

If *feijoada* is a Saturday lunch ritual, the perfect Paulista Sunday follows a *futebol* match with a late pizza supper (more than a million pies are sold in the city on Sundays). And if the wait is eternal at Bráz, the city's best upscale pizzeria? Leave your name at the door and chill with a frosty *chopp* at Bar Original nearby, in the bar-rich southern Moema district. A diminutive pull of draft beer, *chopp* (pronounced *sho*-pee) far outranks the caipirinha as the country's national tipple. "*Chopp* is perhaps more a beachy Rio thing," comments our friend Nirlando Beirão, an elegantly goateed publisher and bon vivant who's just taken us to a Corinthians club soccer match. "But all Brazil is addicted to extremely cold drinks." The cozy, tiled Original elevates draft beer to high science. The brew (small-bubbled Brahma) rests in iceberg-cold tanks for at least two days to settle the head. Wisecracking *chopeiros* chill your glass between ice cubes to precisely 30 degrees before filling it: first beer, then exactly a three-finger thickness of *crema* (foam). Don't stop at just two. Even if rivers of very quaffable Portuguese wine await at Bráz to accompany the ultra-cheesy pies from the infernal wood-burning oven and the pleasantly oily Calabrian sausage bread. Looking up from the puffy round of our chard-and-pine-nut pizza, I notice genial Beirão is brooding. His beloved Corinthians lost.

No brooding—and please, no Havaianas flip-flops, such as I'm wearing—at Gero. Yes, this is the low-key Italian outpost of the chic Fasano hotel and restaurant empire. But according to our table companion—an editor at Brazilian *Vogue*—60 Birkin bags arrived in São Paulo with the opening of the Hermès store, "and

they're all here today." Gero owner Rogério Fasano joins our table, dapper with a cashmere sweater draped just-so over his jacketed shoulders. "Meat smothered in red sauce and cheese, with fries and white rice" is how Fasano describes typical Italo-Brazilian cantina fare. He takes pride in the role his family played in tuning Paulistas to the refinements of modern *cucina*. Fittingly, the porcini in our pasta were flown in from Italy, and the *milanesa*, a plate-size veal cutlet breaded in tiny cubes of white sandwich bread, presents a truly *bella figura*. "São Paulo restaurants are so great because we thrive on regular customers, not a tourist economy," Signor Fasano declares. He then waves *arrivederci* to a regular, the owner of the soccer club São Paulo, the crosstown enemies of the Corinthians.

Subtropical warmth, high-energy urbanism, and Brazilian sexiness blend to deliver a cuisine that dazzles like no other.

In the 21st-century edition of the post-Columbian culinary exchange, Brazilian chefs travel to Spain to absorb new techniques and spread the word about their native ingredients. Meanwhile, Spanish—or rather, Catalan—chefs head to São Paulo, smelling gold. Madrid-based super-toque Sergi Arola opened Arola Vintetres in a high-rise hotel in Jardins. A few years ago the adorable Catalan twins Javier and Sergio Torres (they look like Vince Vaughn's handsomer younger brothers and are chef-owners of the celebrated Dos Cielos, in Barcelona) launched their swank Eñe, in the up-and-coming southern Jardins district. "One of us can always be here, the other in Barcelona," says Sergio, smiling. "Of course nobody can tell us apart." Playing innovation (oyster tartare inside a hollowed-out cherry tomato dolloped with caviar) against tradition (the best *pa amb tomàquet* and *patatas bravas* outside Barcelona), Eñe's menu hits all the right notes. The succulent seafood *fideuà*, a pasta paella, almost transports us to the Spanish Mediterranean *chiringuitos* (beach shacks). Almost, because the room is no shack, with its lipstick-red wall hanging accenting the mod warehouse-style mix of warm wood and concrete.

Surprising but true: São Paulo's 1.5-million-strong Nikkei (Japanese Brazilian) population is the biggest Japanese community outside Japan. This makes the city home to pristine sushi restaurants, such as Jun Sakamoto or Kinu, inside the *muito*-luxe Grand Hyatt hotel. One foggy morning we meet the ebullient Adriano Kanashiro—a third-generation Nikkei of Okinawan descent and owner of the sophisticated sushi restaurant Momotaro—at a street fair in Liberdade, the city's Little Tokyo, near downtown. Japanese first came to Brazil in 1908 to work as farmers, he tells us while sprinkling a springy shrimp ball snagged from a street vendor with *katsuo* flakes and spicy green sauce. "Our ancestral cuisine had to adapt," he continues, now sipping *caju* juice from a tropical-fruit stall, "into its own kind of fusion." To prove his point he swings us by Itiriki Bakery. Here, Japanese *karepan* (curry buns) are sold alongside Brazilian *palmito* cakes and eggy breads laced with Portuguese sausage. Our next stop, Mercado Municipal, the city's main market, is a short drive away. Under its soaring roof we take in the strands of Brazil's multicultural past: Italian purveyors of spicy Calabrian sausage; Portuguese salt cod experts; shrinelike Amazonian stalls hung with herbs used in macumba rituals; riotous produce stands you can smell from miles away. We eyeball an electric-pink wedge of guava while Kanashiro test-chews a new pineapple variety called *gomo-de-mel.* Then he haggles with the fishmonger for crocodile-tail meat. ("Tastes like fish, only fishier.")

Kanashiro is back with us for dinner at the white-hot Kinoshita, where the sushi chefs have Japanese features and sexy Brazilian body language. Kinoshita has a Zen-on-steroids design and a magnetic host in chef and co-owner Tsuyoshi Murakami, Kanashiro's rival and pal. "Mura" was born in Japan and worked in Spain and New York, which explains his beguiling Japo-Mediterranean hybrid cuisine with the occasional tropical flourish. I note that the *umeboshi* plum sauce makes a surprisingly perfect foil for the tangy grilled disks of pupunha, and that buffalo mozzarella benefits from accents of ginger, lime, and house-made soy sauce. This same sweetish organic shoyu mingles with olive oil to highlight a simple, hauntingly delicious dish of daikon and shaved Japanese cured mullet roe. Aha! Across the room I spot an old acquaintance, a Basque chef with a TV show in Spain and a restaurant in Mexico City. He's dining with a famous young Mexican cook whom I last saw in Madrid. Briefly, I join their table. Over mango ravioli with *yuzu* ice, we compare notes from our São Paulo eating adventures. Is *priprioca* the Next Great Flavor? Will Amazonian foodstuffs conquer the world? We share in the feeling: the future is now. ✦

GUIDE

EAT

A Figueira Rubaiyat
1738 Rua Haddock Lobo;
55-11/3087-1399;
rubaiyat.com.br. **$$$$**

Bar Original
137 Rua Graúna;
55-11/5093-9486;
baroriginal.com.br. **$$**

Bráz
125 Rua Graúna;
55-11/5561-1736. **$$$**

Dalva e Dito
1115 Rua Padre João Manuel;
55-11/3064-4444;
dalvaedito.com.br. **$$$**

D.O.M.
549 Rua Barão de Capanema;
55-11/3088-0761;
domrestaurante.com.br.
$$$$

Eñe
213 Rua Dr. Mario Ferraz;
55-11/3816-4333;
enerestaurante.com.br. **$$$**

Gero
1629 Rua Haddock Lobo;
55-11/3064-0005;
fasano.com.br. **$$$**

Itiriki Bakery
24 Rua dos Estudantes;

55-11/3277-4939;
bakeryitiriki.com.

Kinoshita
405 Rua Jacques Félix;
55-11/3849-6940;
restaurantekinoshita.com.br.
$$$$

Kinu
13301 Avda. Nações Unidas;
55-11/2838-3207;
restaurantejapones-kinu.
com.br. **$$$$**

Maní
210 Rua Joaquim Antunes;
55-11/3085-4148;
manimanioca.com.br. **$$$**

Mercado Municipal
306 Rua da Cantareira;
55-11/3313-3365;
mercadomunicipal.com.br.

Mocotó
1100 Avda. Nossa Senhora do
Loreto; 55-11/2951-3056;
mocoto.com.br. **$$$**

Momotaro
591 Rua Diogo Jacome;
55-11/3842-5590;
restaurantemomotaro.com.br.
$$$

Pão de Queijo
Haddock Lobo
1408 Rua Haddock Lobo;
55-11/3088-3087.

Sipping a
jaboticaba
caipirinha at
Mocotó.
Right: Eñe's
kitchen.

Mocotó's
tapioca flan.
Left: The
dining room
and lounge
at Maní.

Du Pain et des Idées, a traditional Parisian *boulangerie.*

Europe

The exterior of
Quo Vadis, in London's
Soho. Opposite: The
restaurant's duck-and-
pheasant pot pie.

London Is the Capital of Food

BY PETER JON LINDBERG / PHOTOGRAPHED BY JASON LOWE

A honky-tonk roadhouse serving deep-fried pickles and chili-cheese fries. A Parsi café straight out of old Bombay. A semi-secret chef's table, tucked behind a hot dog joint, that's giving Copenhagen a run for its foraged nettles. If you haven't eaten in London lately, get back as soon as you can—and expect the unexpected. Over the past six months I've made multiple visits to the city, running the gamut of its ever-expanding food scene. My focus was on new or recent openings, along with a few old favorites still going strong. As I crisscrossed the city, three things became apparent.

One: you can travel a long way to eat at a great local restaurant here. (On, Bermondsey, Clapham, Hackney, and Brixton!) Today's standouts are often in neighborhoods well beyond the West End. You could liken it to the Brooklyn effect in New York, but a proper comparison would have to throw in the Bronx, Staten Island, and New Jersey as well. Still, central London is far from over: Soho is enjoying its umpteenth revival, and Covent Garden is suddenly red-hot for dining. Meanwhile, the buzz has shifted to such once-humdrum enclaves as Marylebone and Fitzrovia—the latter home to two of the city's best restaurants. (More on that later.)

Two: there is no "London dining scene," in the singular sense. Though certain tropes and trends pop up, there's little to unify the city's food offerings, except that the bill is calculated in pounds sterling. As with music and fashion, the culinary realm here has been niched and sub-niched so much that the options are now near-endless.

Three: few cities on earth offer food this good across the board. That's not a judgment; it's a fact. Pound for pound, nose to tail, there's never been a better—or, frankly, wackier—time to eat here. So which London are you after?

The City of Amazing Breakfasts

What a drag to live in London and have a job—a dreary morning-interrupter that keeps you from lingering over the day's best meal. Options are myriad: Tom's Kitchen for the full English, Daylesford for poached eggs, the Wolseley for every damn thing on the menu. But Granger & Co. is not only the prettiest breakfast spot in town, it's arguably the best. Opened by Australian chef Bill Granger, whose Sydney café Bills is legendary for eggs and pancakes, it occupies a prime block of Notting Hill where geraniums fill every window box. Sunlight pours through double-height windows, casting a glow on the radiant crowd, most of whom look as if they've come from a morning swim at Bondi. Order an Aussie-style flat white, grab a paper from the granite-topped bar, and indulge in a platter of silky eggs, gently folded with I don't want to fathom how much cream, and served with chipolata sausages and avocado relish—or go all out for Granger's famous ricotta hotcakes, topped with sticky, molten chunks of honeycomb butter.

For a more old-world vibe, head to Sloane Square and join the air-kissers at Colbert, from Chris Corbin and Jeremy King, the gifted duo behind the indefatigable Wolseley. They've taken over the corner spot long occupied by Oriel, whose food was so lousy that the building's landlord, the Earl of Cadogan, purportedly refused to renew the lease. He turned the space over to Corbin and King, who upgraded it in the manner of an all-day Parisian grand café. With stage-set lighting, Buñuel posters, and impeccably distressed mirrors, Colbert could coast by on looks alone. Yet as at the Wolseley, the food is way better than it has to

Chef Ollie Dabbous. Left: Smoked-salmon sandwiches from Maltby Street Market.

The Maltby Street Market. Right: Inside Dishoom Shoreditch.

Damien Hirst's *Cock and Bull* installation, at Tramshed.

be. Order the champagne-rhubarb compote atop thick, tangy Greek yogurt with a side of nutty house-made granola, and your day will be the better for it.

The City of a Million Markets

More than Paris, New York, or even Tokyo, this is a city devoted to the pleasure of ogling foodstuffs—from the gorgeous *fattoush* salads at Ottolenghi to the hunks of Stichelton at La Fromagerie, labeled in dainty farmer's script. Yes, London can be insanely overpriced, and at times comically precious. (When I dropped into the Albion, the Conran café in Shoreditch, the adjacent grocery was selling seagull eggs "collected by licensed pickers on Hampshire marshes.") Yet for sheer quality of ingredients, London is hard to top. This is the land of great milk and better honey, where egg yolks bear the color of Thai monks' robes.

Then there are the weekend markets, with their bins of Romanesco and steel-drum-size pans of paella. Borough Market is the big one, of course. But an upstart has laid claim to the throne. Tucked under the smoke-stained Victorian railway arches running through an industrial patch of Bermondsey, the weekend-only Maltby Street Market was founded in 2010 by defectors from Borough. It's quickly become London's hottest block party. On a recent visit, the Comptoir Gourmand was selling giant pink-and-white meringues resembling pashas' turbans; at Tozino, two young Spaniards were carving *jamón ibérico* to order. St. John Bakery was making open-faced sandwiches with Faeroe Islands salmon from the North London outfit Hansen & Lydersen, which cold-smokes the fish over beechwood and juniper. Down the lane at Christchurch Fish, an Albert Finney ringer was shucking oysters for a queue of 20. Most took their edible prizes over to the Little Bird Gin Bar, Maltby's de facto hub, run by the small-batch London gin maker of the same name. Owner Tim Moore started in the spring of 2012 with just a folding table and sample-size cocktails—but as the crowds grew, so did the concept. "Suddenly, we were running a proper bar," he says, still bemused. Intended or not, it works: mismatched chairs cluster around wobbly tables topped with fresh-cut flowers in gin bottles. Birdcages hang from the archways. And bearded lads in jaunty thrift-store caps serve negronis and Aviations in vintage crystal coupes. Can your market do that?

The City Whose Patron Saint Is John

With all respect to Ramsay, White, and Blumenthal, if there's one British chef whose influence currently ranks above all others, it's the inimitable Fergus Henderson, whose St. John empire has nonetheless spawned countless imitations. With its throwback-British cooking and ascetic shirking of pretense—in the dining room and on the plate—St. John was an outlier in the flashy, fusion-prone nineties. Today, its disciples are legion. And nearly two decades on, the original St. John still kills it out in Clerkenwell. For my money, I'll take a long boozy lunch at St. John Bread & Wine, in Spitalfields, with the pale English sun streaming into a room like a public-school caff: rows of coat hooks, a blackboard, a grid of scratched wooden tables. The chummy English waiter waxes poetic about the veal chop, then brings you currant-filled Eccles cake for dessert, which he calls pudding.

It was Henderson, of course, who made London safe again for offal; now every other kitchen in town serves calves' tongues and duck hearts—and, righteous as nose-to-tail eating may be, it can get a bit same-y after a while. (A man tired of London isn't necessarily tired of life; he may just be weary of lambs' brains.) But St. John also helped revive those defiantly British, deceptively simple dishes one's great-aunt in Leeds might crave, from smoked eel to potted shrimps. Such are the draws at the relaunched Quo Vadis, the clubby Soho landmark that's stepped up tenfold since chef Jeremy Lee took over last year. Spread across several snug, low-ceilinged dining rooms, it's a convivial spot, with a nursery's worth of greenery and a menu that could have been

conceived and typeset in 1876. Bring yourself to order "bloater paste" and you'll be rewarded with a sumptuous herring pâté topped with a tasty layer of congealed butter to be pierced by a shard of crusty bread. And Lee's smoked-eel sandwich, served on grilled sourdough bread with pickled onions and creamy horseradish, is fantastic (and, it turns out, a favorite of Henderson's).

Trad-British simplicity is also on the menu at Mark Hix's Tramshed, located on funky Rivington Street in Shoreditch. You have two choices: grilled sirloin, priced by the gram, or a whole roasted free-range chicken. You want the latter; the steak is just fine, but the bird is close to perfect, its skin crisp and its meat delicate and juicy, all the better when dipped in fiery English mustard. And the setting? A gorgeously decayed trolley shed, built in 1905, with hulking steel girders rising three stories to a soaring, skylit ceiling. The coup de grâce: a Damien Hirst installation of a bull, encased in formaldehyde, with a rooster perched on its back.

The City Where We're All Well-Fed French Peasants

St. John's influence extends to places where the food isn't even particularly British. Ed Wilson and Oli Barker work in a similarly robust, offal-y vein, but take their cue from the rustic *campagnard* cooking of France. They've built a small empire of their own with Terroirs (a natural-wine bar near Covent Garden), Brawn (a temple to pork in Bethnal Green), the Green Man & French Horn (focused on the wine and food of the Loire Valley), and the excellent new Soif, which their British clientele pronounces "Soyf."

Soif sits on a remote stretch of Battersea Rise that bears all the marks of hipsterfication: women with Feist bangs; guys in stevedore caps. The narrow room is decked out with old wine barrels and French bric-a-brac; the menu makes any season feel like winter. Ribbons of melt-on-the-tongue *fromage de tête* come dressed with cornichon-spiked vinaigrette and adorned with a soft-cooked egg, the yolk glowing like a sunset. A luxuriantly creamy soup of Jerusalem artichokes is festooned with petals of meaty, umami-rich black trumpet mushrooms. Basile, the sommelier—a Gallic Ethan Hawke—can walk you through the list of more than 200 wines, only a handful of which aren't natural or biodynamic. Remember when Brits drank mostly claret? They don't, either.

The City Obsessed with Tapas

Is there any *jamon ibérico* left in Spain? You'd guess not, based on the number of tapas bars in London, each with a glistening ham racked up on the countertop. Long is the love the British have for the Iberian peninsula—and that love is begetting ever-better rewards. Worthy newcomers include the Basque-devoted Donostia, in plummy Marylebone, whose chef Damian Surowiec prepares classics like blistered Padrón peppers with sea salt and roasted pork shoulder with a nutty *romesco* sauce.

Meanwhile, in Bermondsey—a slum in *Oliver Twist*, now a tony arts-and-media enclave—the Spanish chef José Pizarro has opened Pizarro, the larger offshoot to his popular tapas bar José. The new space is even more rustic-chic: plank floors, unfinished beams, industrial desk lamps, and reclaimed chandeliers. Settle into a half-moon banquette, order a bottle of Txakoli (which your server will pour, per custom, from a height), and don't stop till you've tried the entire tapas menu. You'll want the girolle mushrooms with batons of Manchego in truffle oil, flecked with parsley and chives. You'll definitely need the razor clams, impossibly tender and drizzled with strong, grassy olive oil. And you mustn't miss the chopped salmon: lightly cured in beet juice and crowned with an egg yolk to mix in à la tartare. (Egg yolks are everywhere these days; they are the ampersands of contemporary London.)

The City That Can Out-India India

Bengali prawns, Hyderabadi biryani, Karnatakan *dosai*... if it's cooked somewhere in India, it's served somewhere in London, where thousands of South Asian restaurants specialize in countless regional cuisines. One thing you couldn't find much of till now: the Parsi cooking of Bombay's beloved Irani cafés. In the 1960's, Bombay had hundreds of such places—elegantly worn rooms with faded tile floors, creaking fans, and a devoted clientele that transcended class and caste. Now only a few dozen remain. All of which makes the charming Dishoom, in Shoreditch, (a follow-up to the sleeker Covent Garden original) such a find. An uncanny homage to Bombay's Britannia—the king of Irani cafés—the place feels like

Cranberry biryani from Dishoom. Below: A waitress at Meat Liquor.

a walk-in sepia photograph, bathed in dreamy light from Deco sconces and lamps fashioned from antique film projectors. Archival photos and old Hindi adverts capture the funky glamour of midcentury Bombay.

But Dishoom isn't just a movie-set simulacrum; it also serves terrific food. Consider its take on berry *pulao*, the tart Parsi-style biryani. I've long pined for one equal to Britannia's, and Dishoom's intricately flavored variation—made with tangy cranberries instead of barberries—comes as close as any. There's also a deep, rich, black-lentil dal, fragrant with wintery spice, into which I kept swirling spoonfuls of yogurt to create spirals of creamy deliciousness. For those who really miss Mumbai, Dishoom even serves Thums Up, the Indian Coke. Never again should one settle for generic curry on nearby Brick Lane.

The City That Ate America

London is right now in thrall to at least a dozen different food crazes, among them a rage for old-school steak houses, a burgeoning Peruvian trend, a sudden wave of authentic Mexican, and a welcome influx of great Vietnamese (the chic new Cây Tre Soho has fabulous *bánh cuón* ravioli and a knockout ox-cheek *pho*). But of all the exotic foods making their way to these shores, the least likely is also the most pervasive: London has gone mad for American junk food.

You can't swing a Welsh corgi around here without hitting some jam-packed burger, hot dog, fried-chicken, or barbecue joint. Just off Carnaby Street, Pitt Cue started life as a truck before going brick-and-mortar in 2012. The pit master does impressive work with smoky, slow-cooked beef ribs, and the addictive mashed potatoes come laced with marrow and a sticky glaze of barbecue drippings. (Chase it with an A&W root beer.) Eight blocks east is the new Soho branch of Brixton-based Honest Burgers, which sources rare-breed North Yorkshire beef from Ginger Pig, the city's best butcher. The namesake burger is excellent: an inch-thick patty of savory dry-aged chuck, cooked to a properly pink medium and topped with onion relish, lettuce, pickles, bacon, and aged cheddar. Better still are the crisp twice-cooked fries sprinkled with rosemary salt. Meanwhile, in Fitzrovia, the red-hot Bubbledogs pairs grower champagnes with gussied-up hot dogs (including a *bánh*

mì variation with pickled carrots, fennel, cucumber, cauliflower, and Sriracha-spiced mayo).

Then there's Meat Liquor, currently the trendiest restaurant in London. Join the epic queue, cross the velvet rope, and step inside a faux roadhouse soaked in graffiti and blood-red neon. The sound track is raunchy psychobilly; the food pure, uncut Amurrican. The saucy, spicy "dead hippie" burger is justly revered as one of London's best, with a good bun-to-filling ratio and a satisfying if sloppy integrity. A reckless man might side it with deep-fried pickles. As my eyes adjusted to the dim, I noticed an absurdly gorgeous quartet of male and female models—all with butterscotch English accents—noshing on chili-cheese fries and chugging PBR.

The City of Earthy Delights

By now you've surely heard the hype about Dabbous, the 12-table room in Fitzrovia run by 32-year-old chef Ollie Dabbous, who's earned second-coming-like praise since his debut in 2012. (Given that London critics are the nastiest on the planet, this is no small feat.) I can report that the food really is that good, even if the space comes off like an assembly-line floor—all concrete, steel, and exposed ductwork. You expect to be issued a welder's apron. The servers, however, are amiable and informed, and what the room lacks in color is made up for on the plates. A startlingly vivid pea-and-mint starter celebrates the miracle of England's greatest ingredient: a bright-green pea purée, drizzled with tart pea oil, topped with minty pea granita and whole peas in the shell, their tangly shoots climbing up the rim. It is the greenest dish you've ever seen, a bowlful of emeralds. You want a spatula to scoop up every bite.

Dabbous' signature dish, a coddled egg with smoked butter and wild mushrooms, arrives in the shell perched on a nest of straw. Imagine a Japanese *chawanmushi* custard, but tasting definitively of the English soil. It is unspeakably delicious. Even the bread course is unexpected: a house-made seeded sourdough redolent of...smoky bacon. (After baking, the bread is cooled on a rack above a barbecuing *ibérico* ham.)

One can imagine the chef as a boy, playing in some rustling meadow or English garden, conducting experiments on all that grows there. His kitchen does much the same: pickling rose petals, transforming pine needles into a heady consommé, mixing horseradish with buttermilk, fashioning nests of hay, garnishing each dazzling creation with edible flowers. It's an astonishingly assured restaurant, and I urge you to try it yourself, if you can score a table—I hear there are a few left for 2014.

The City You Never Expected
Much as I loved Dabbous, the place I keep dreaming about is two blocks farther north—hidden, as it happens, behind the aforementioned Bubbledogs. It's called Kitchen Table, and it served me one of the finest meals in my memory.

Chef James Knappett and his wife, sommelier Sandia Chang, make a nice emblem for the new England: he, a Noma- and Per Se–trained Brit; she, a Saudi-born Asian American schooled in Los Angeles. They met in New York, moved to London, and started Bubbledogs last summer. But it's in the back room, at Kitchen Table, that Knappett does his finest work: creating a 10- to 14-course, daily-changing tasting menu for 19 diners who sit at a zinc countertop around the open kitchen.

Opera plays softly in the background; the nighttime clamor at Bubbledogs is just a faint buzz beyond the curtain. Chang pours champagne while Knappett and three sous-chefs work the stoves. The hand-lettered menu lists just a single word for each course (BURRATA/ PHEASANT/PASTA/PIG), playing up the surprise. First up: a plump Cornish shrimp, served raw, with fresh dill and frozen horseradish. It is luscious, elemental, sensational. The chatter of the room drops to a hush as we all realize what we're in for: attention must be paid. Knappett, meanwhile, is as humble as can be, introducing each course himself and charming his guests with funny stories. He confesses to nearly being arrested while foraging for sorrel and nettles on national parkland ("The cop said, 'I have no idea why anyone would want to eat this stuff, so I'm going to look the other way— but don't ever come back here again' "). He rhapsodizes about the 32 varieties of herbs growing "at my mum's place" in Cambridgeshire, including the verbena that perfumes the sauce for the Scottish lobster. He raves about the samphire he collected on the coast of Cornwall and the English—yes, English—truffles he sources from "a top-secret woodland" in Wiltshire.

A coddled egg with mushrooms and smoked butter at Dabbous.

In an era when restaurant cooking is about too many hands doing too much with your food or too few doing far too little, Kitchen Table finds a laudable balance. The pheasant course, for instance: confited leg meat, mixed with thyme and pickled rhubarb, then rolled in delicate *brik* pastry and deep-fried, like a Moroccan cigar. It rests on a silky purée of Jerusalem artichokes alongside stewed bonbon dates, and is scattered with puffed barley. The result is ingenious: complex yet comforting, novel yet deeply familiar.

While Knappett explains each dish, his sous-chefs are already assembling the next course, like stagehands in the wings, offering us tantalizing glimpses of what's to come: a snow-white turbot fillet here, a tangle of sea purslane there. The cooks are remarkably young—average age 24—but maintain intense focus, working hard to create a sense of play. After three hours the night is winding down, and the kitchen crew begins to relax and joke around. Strangely, no one seems tired, least of all the guests. Despite the forest of empty wine glasses before us, we're feeling rather energized. So much so that I'm tempted to order another round of the pheasant. ✦

Maltby Street Market's Little Bird Gin Bar.

GUIDE

EAT

The Albion
2-4 Boundary St., Shoreditch;
44-20/7729-1051;
albioncaff.co.uk. $$$

Bubbledogs
70 Charlotte St., Fitzrovia;
44-20/7637-7770;
bubbledogs.co.uk. $$

Cây Tre Soho
42-43 Dean St., Soho;
44-20/7317-9118;
caytresoho.co.uk. $$$

Colbert
50-52 Sloane Square,
Chelsea; 44-20/7730-2804;
colbertchelsea.com. $$$

Dabbous
39 Whitfield St., Fitzrovia;
44-20/7730-2804;
dabbous.co.uk. $$$

Daylesford
44B Pimlico Rd., Belgravia;
44-20/7881-8060;
daylesfordorganic.com. $$$

Dishoom Shoreditch
7 Boundary St., Shoreditch;
44-20/7420-9324;
dishoom.com. $$

Donostia
10 Seymour Place,
Marylebone; 44-20/3620-
1845; donostia.co.uk. $$

Granger & Co.
175 Westbourne Grove,
Notting Hill; 44-20/7229-
8944; grangerandco.com. $$

Honest Burgers
4A Meard St., Soho;
44-20/3609-9524;
honestburgers.co.uk. $$

**Kitchen Table @
Bubbledogs**
70 Charlotte St., Fitzrovia;
44-20/7637-7770; kitchen
tablelondon.co.uk. $$$$

Maltby Street Market
Maltby St., Bermondsey;
maltby.st; weekends
10 a.m.–4 p.m.

Meat Liquor
74 Welbeck St., Marylebone;
44-20/7224-4239;
meatliquor.com. $$

Pitt Cue
1 Newburgh St., Soho;
44-20/7287-5578;
pittcue.co.uk. $$

Pizarro
194 Bermondsey St.,
Southwark; 44-20/7378-
9455; josepizarro.com. $$$

Quo Vadis
26-29 Dean St., Soho;
44-20/7437-9585;
quovadissoho.co.uk. $$$

Soif
27 Battersea Rise, Clapham;
44-20/7223-1112;
soif.co. $$$

St. John
26 St. John St., Clerkenwell;
44-20/7251-0848;
stjohngroup.uk.com. $$$

St. John Bread & Wine
94-96 Commercial St.,
Spitalfields;
44-20/7251-0848;
stjohngroup.uk.com. $$

Tom's Kitchen
27 Cale St., Chelsea;
44-20/7349-0202;
tomskitchen.co.uk. $$

Tramshed
32 Rivington St., Shoreditch;
44-20/7749-0478;
chickenandsteak.co.uk. $$$

The Wolseley
160 Piccadilly, St. James's;
44-20/7499-6996;
thewolseley.com. $$$

Barcelona

The Spanish are unyieldingly democratic when it comes to dining. Consider Barcelona, where clued-in locals are as likely to eat at a temple of molecular gastronomy as they are at a no-frills tapas joint. That's because the food at both is shockingly good. Read on for the city's top tables.

Abac Restaurant & Hotel

In one of Barcelona's chicest boutique hotels, wood-walled Abac Restaurant has been a power-lunch destination ever since chef Jordi Cruz earned it a second Michelin star in 2012. Deconstructed neo-Catalan cuisine is the draw here, from the raw *hamachi* with cherries and cucumber snow to the violet ice cream. Fittingly, both courses arrive at the table on Versace-designed plates. *1 Avinguda del Tibidabo; 34/93-319-6600; abacbarcelona.com.* **$$$$**

Alkimia

Chef Jordi Vilà specializes in cerebral, offbeat takes on regional dishes at the white-on-white Alkimia. What to order? The umami-rich veal kidney with coffee crumbs or broiled crawfish with saffron and rice, accompanied by a glass of fruity Tempranillo from the expansive wine selection. *79 Carr. de la Indústria; 34/93-207-6115; alkimia.cat.* **$$$**

Can Maño

It doesn't look like much from the outside, but Can Maño, a modest seafood canteen in La Barceloneta, is a neighborhood favorite. Die-hard regulars line up for staples such as fried artichokes, calamari, and fresh-caught mackerel, then wash them down with amber-colored Moscatel wine. *12 Carr. del Baluard; 34/93-319-3082.* **$$**

Fàbrica Moritz Barcelona

Your average microbrewery this is not. Architect Jean Nouvel renovated the 19th-century beer factory, combining 150-year-old brickwork with modern touches such as colored-glass-paneled walls. A happy-hour crowd fills the bar each evening as much for the food as for the drinks. Opt for the *flammkuchen,* an Alsatian-style pizza topped with Muenster cheese, crème fraîche, bacon, and slim-cut sausage, and traditional *patatas bravas* (fried potatoes) with creamy aioli. *41 Ronda Sant Antoni; 34/93-426-0050.* **$$**

Pakta

On the heels of their wildly popular tapas spot Tickets (think algae tempura and "liquid olives," made by spherifying the fruit's purée), Ferran Adrià and his brother Albert take an international turn at Pakta. Expect a 35-course degustation menu of creative Peruvian-Japanese tapas: salmon *causa* (mashed potatoes topped with raw fish), tuna *nigiri* with an *ají* pepper sauce, and sashimi-like sea bass *tiraditos,* served in a kumquat marinade. For dessert, don't miss the *picarones* (fig-and-sweet-potato doughnuts). *5 Carr. Lérida.* **$$$**

Quimet & Quimet

Patrons stand elbow to elbow at the stainless-steel counter of Quimet & Quimet, a bustling fifth-generation bar. Request the *mojama* (shaved dried tuna), bacalao (salt cod), and Tou dels Tillers cheese. Or try the mussels paired with sweet tomato jam and a glass of the restaurant's namesake beer. *25 Carr. del Poeta Cabanyes; 34/93-442-3142.* **$$**

Sagàs Pagesos, Cuiners & Co.

The organic ingredients served at this rustic-chic dining room come from chef-owner Oriol Rovira's nearby farm, but the recipes are globally inspired, from the succulent *bo ssäm* (Korean pork buns) and Mexican *chicharrones* to the *cuajada,* a tangy sheep-milk curd with rosemary honey. *13 Pla de Palau; 34/93-343-5410; sagaspagesosicuiners.com.* **$$**

Speakeasy

You'll have to wander through the kitchen to reach the clandestine Speakeasy, owner Javier de las Muelas's ode to 1920's Chicago, housed in an old warehouse in the Eixample district. Tuck in to a plate of briny oysters or crisp suckling pig while jazz plays in the background; then head to the dimly lit cocktail bar, where a tuxedo-clad bartender will prepare you a flawless martini—or two. *162 Carr. d'Aribau; 34/93-217-5080; javierdelasmuelas.com.* **$$$**

Tapas, 24

Chef Carles Abellan brings El Bulli chops to his popular Eixample staple. Baskets of fresh produce line the counters of an open-air kitchen that turns out small plates from morning till midnight: *huevos estrellados con chorizo* (eggs, fried potatoes, and sausage); truffle-laced ham-and-cheese sandwiches; and decadent chocolate ganache sprinkled with Maldon sea salt and spread over toasted bread. But it's the savory foie gras burger that keeps devotees coming back. *269 Carr. de la Diputació; 34/93-488-0977; projectes24.com.* **$$**

The bar at Quimet & Quimet. Right: Chef Jordi Cruz of Abac Restaurant & Hotel.

Pakta's bar area. Left: Grilled chicken wings and fried Padrón peppers at Tapas, 24.

The Christianshavns canal
in central Copenhagen.
Opposite: Grilled
onions with gooseberry
blossoms at Noma.

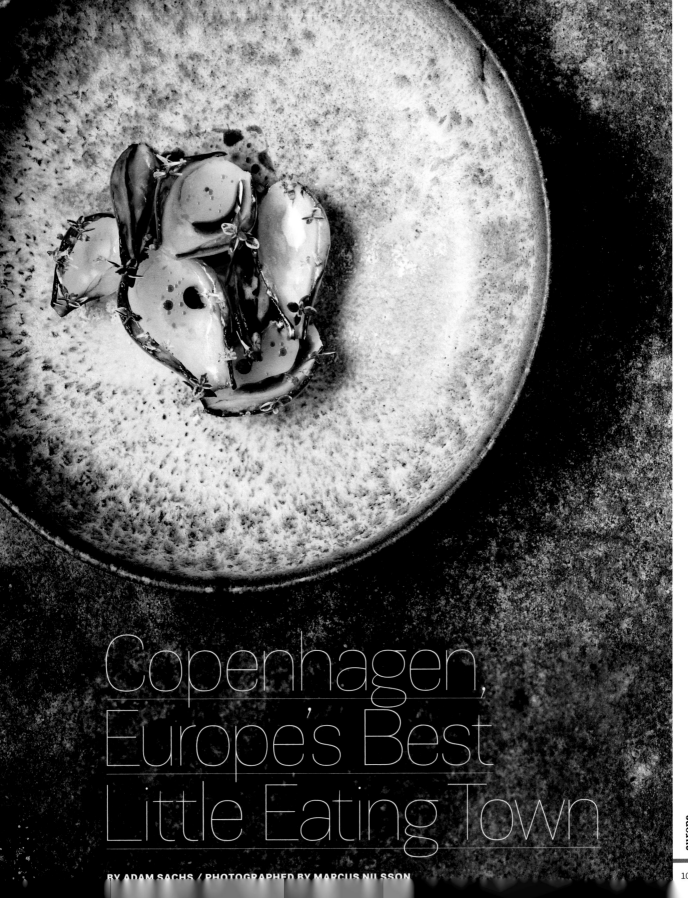

Copenhagen, Europe's Best Little Eating Town

BY ADAM SACHS / PHOTOGRAPHED BY MARCUS NILSSON

Chef Christian Puglisi at his Restaurant Relæ. Left: Noma's quayside home.

Relæ's dining room. Right: A hearty breakfast at Manfreds & Vin.

magine you are a mushroom. What do you dream of? In the not-so-distant past, the lucky few would have been shipped off to France and pressed into the service of haute cuisine, minced into a dainty duxelles. Or perhaps would have gone out in style, drowned in cream and Cognac. But the world of fine dining has changed while you've been lazing in the shade, mushroom. You're the main event now. (Suck it, rib eye.) You're a hen of the woods. A gnarled, noble, many-limbed and meaty beast, growing fat as an actual chicken on the cold Danish forest floor. Here comes a famous foraging chef to pluck you from obscurity, tote you gingerly back to his kitchen, age you like a steak,

and make you a star. Two weeks of rest deepens your fungal funk. Now you're ready to be pan-roasted and presented whole tableside. Shown off like some truffle-studded *poulet de Bresse* or the finest Dover sole. You sit on an inky purée of Gotland truffles and rich mushroom broth. You're adorned with a garland of shaved truffles and crunchy blades of wild sorrel. This is the life, baby. You ain't just a salad or a side dish anymore! The crusading chef and ennobler of vegetables in question is, of course, René Redzepi. His restaurant is Noma, in the dockside Christianshavn district of Copenhagen, Denmark. Redzepi has become well-known in the past few years for doing things like slowly sautéing winter-hardened year-old "vintage" carrots from the marshy fields of Lammefjord in goat's butter and chamomile. Or serving a plump and perfect shelled langoustine clinging to the face of a large, warm stone—as if it had just washed ashore on this rock dotted with barnacles made of emulsified oyster and parsley and dusted with toasted rye.

You'd need to have been living under one of these beach stones to have missed the news: Noma is the best restaurant in the world. Actually, it works better if you shout it: THE BEST RESTAURANT IN THE WORLD! Then imagine an entire country of beaming Danes high-fiving each other from the upright seats of their fixed-gear bicycles, looking even more apple-cheeked, well-adjusted, and handsome

than they normally do, while in other quarters of the Continent, the French shrug long-sufferingly and disgruntled Spaniards shake their fists and rattle their nitrous-oxide canisters, wondering who this northern upstart is that's stolen their culinary limelight.

For three years running, Noma has held the top ranking in the San Pellegrino World's 50 Best Restaurants list, a poll of international opinion-shapers and professional food nerds (full disclosure: I vote in the thing). Redzepi's trick is balancing rigorous austerity with freewheeling deliciousness. It's fun and it's weird and it's never, even for a moment, dull or preachy in the way that restaurants with lofty goals (and loftier self-regard) often are. The beams in the spare dining room show their age; gray, mottled, and unadorned. The silverware fails to impress with its gleam or heft. In fact, a dozen small courses may pass before you're presented with so much as a fork. There is a serenity here achieved without the benefit of velvety acres of plush carpeting. No gilded cheese trolley. No courtly waiters in dinner jackets. The chefs deliver the food they've made to the table themselves, introducing each dish with unscripted enthusiasm.

At lunch recently, Redzepi came by the table to explain a little plate of battered and fried leek ends—roots and all. "This is an example of what we call 'trash cooking,'" he said. "By necessity, during a hard winter, we started thinking about what to do with the things in a kitchen you'd normally throw away."

Of course the idea of crowning any one restaurant as the world's best is a little goofy. One man's trash cooking is, after all, another man's garbage. Still, what's important is that Redzepi and his team have conjured up that honest rarity: the new thing that isn't mere novelty. And they did it not by trying to appeal to the exacting standards of the Michelin inspector, not by making things ever more fancy and unapproachable, but by returning to the edible topography of Scandinavia and making something beautiful of the overlooked roots, sturdy weeds, and cold-water sea creatures he found there.

There's an anti-fussy elegance to the new Nordic approach, and I hope it's catching.

In doing so he grabbed the attention of the gastro-tourists and wandering food writers and poll-takers alike. Praise and attention are heaped on the 34-year-old chef in the liberal manner that herring here is piled onto smørrebrød. More importantly, the success of Noma has inspired and challenged his fellow chefs—and changed the way the city eats.

Now Redzepi's cooks are spreading through town, opening places of their own and trying on new styles. The first flush of Noma imitators seems to have died down (there is only so much edible dirt people can eat). And outside forces such as the financial crisis have led some big-name chefs to close their ambitious expense-account dining rooms and open more casual, populist restaurants. Redzepi told me he'd seen wild ramson leaves in a Copenhagen supermarket, something unthinkable in Denmark a few years ago. I wouldn't know a ramson if I stepped on it, but I got his point: the Nordic culinary revolution is real and ongoing. It's an ideal time to visit what's arguably the most exciting place to eat in Europe right now, a city enjoying its time in the spotlight and busy figuring out what comes next.

The nicest way to reach the cobblestoned street of Jægersborggade is to cut through the leafy lanes of Assistens Cemetery. Grumpy Kierkegaard is buried here, as is the immortally smooth American saxophonist Ben Webster. More transient visitors sunbathe between the cherry trees. The place is, like the whole city, designed for civic enjoyment, practical cycling, and leisurely strolling.

There's a hand-painted sign pointing up and down Jægersborggade. Food and art this way, wine and ceramics over here. You could probably find the Coffee Collective without the sign. Look for the bikes parked out front and follow the strong smell of good coffee into the phone-booth-size space. They roast their own beans here (from Panama, Brazil, Guatemala, and Kenya). Sitting in the sun and sipping espresso at the picnic table outside, it's hard to imagine this was once a derelict block run by hash dealers.

It wasn't until two ex-Noma guys, Christian Puglisi and Kim Rossen, opened a small place called Restaurant Relæ that the neighborhood began to change.

Before long, people on pilgrimage to Noma heard about its ex-sous-chef doing inventive stuff in an unfashionable part of town. Locals jammed the place every night. Puglisi next opened Manfreds, a wine bar and casual all-day restaurant across the street, and now there was a place on the block to get a bottle of natural wine and stick around after dinner. Redzepi's business partner, Claus Meyer, opened Meyers Bageri. The bakery, which makes bread and pastries from organic flour they produce themselves, stands opposite the Coffee Collective as a perfect breakfast counterpart: two small places doing a narrow range of things remarkably well.

You could easily justify a day of eating your way up and down Jægersborggade. Stop for espressos at the picnic table outside the Coffee Collective, cross the street for some knotty cinnamon rolls, cross back, repeat. Make some time to visit Keramiker Inge Vincents, whose diaphanous ceramics are used at Relæ. The one thing you can't get on the street anymore is hash. City officials took notice of how much business the Noma diaspora was bringing to a formerly unkempt area. Dining trumped drugs and the cops chased the pushers off Jægersborggade. (I hear they've relocated to a nearby park. No hard feelings.)

Noma's sous-chefs prepare a tartare of beef and wood sorrel. Below: The blackboard takeaway menu at Manfreds & Vin.

"Fuck what they're doing in France," Puglisi says. Except it's hard to get across how affable and gentle he sounds as he says it. Puglisi is half Sicilian, half Norwegian, raised mostly in Denmark, and a model specimen of the current crop of Copenhagen restaurateurs: young, entrepreneurial, loyal to Redzepi but eager to blaze his own trail. What he learned at Noma, what he calls "the dogmatic Nordic approach," was to create lighter dishes, use more vegetables, more acidity, less dependence on veal stock and other building blocks of classic fine dining. "But the most important thing that Noma is teaching us is to do our own thing. Not everyone has to forage and use sea buckthorn and pine needles. The point is to do something that other people don't and make it what you want it to be."

For Puglisi that has meant cooking original food that doesn't fit any particular label and having fun doing it. Relæ has three set menus a night, one of them vegetarian. Johnny Cash is on the stereo. The tiny open kitchen is full of silent orchestrated mayhem. First on the vegetable menu is an orb of sheep's-milk yogurt enveloping bites of turnip. Layered over the yogurt, stems up, is a covering of green nasturtium leaves. It's all seemingly so simple, but then again it isn't: the piquant yogurt whipped with a little cream into a supple mousse; the bright, surprising, peppery spice delivered by the nasturtium; the turnips mellowed by cooking but still retaining a welcome crunch. It's a dish to make you love a vegetable menu, and one that exemplifies Puglisi's dictum: for a small kitchen to turn out thoughtful, engaging food at a decent price, you have to think as much about the flavors and composition of a dish as you would at a restaurant like Noma—then find ways to make them dead simple to get on the plate. "I don't want a Michelin-starred restaurant with that kind of rhythm. I want something crazy busy. I want it to be hammering."

I tried several times to make a dinner reservation at Radio but that wasn't possible. I tried to make a lunch reservation but again, no luck. Finally the online reservation grid opened, though just a crack. Precisely one seat was available that week at 1 p.m. on Saturday, which is precisely when I showed up to find the place completely empty.

A barista at the
Coffee Collective
stand in the
Torvehallerne KBH
food market.

"Adam?" the waiter warmly smiled when I poked my head in the door, wondering if I'd arrived on the wrong day. He explained that they intentionally limit the crowd at lunch. "We don't want to be stressed all the time!" the waiter said. And it was true, he didn't seem stressed at all. Today they'd decided to take just a dozen reservations. The other 11 would be here shortly.

Radio is small and wood-paneled and pleasant. Johnny Cash was on the stereo here, too, singing "Bridge over Troubled Water," a song I'd never heard him cover. Maybe he only sings it in Danish restaurants, where it seems he is in eternal demand. Claus Meyer is a partner here, too, which explains the reach and undeniable popularity of what is, to all appearances, a tidy little neighborhood joint. The restaurant has a two-acre patch of organically farmed land outside the city that supplies most of its vegetables, and it sources wild meat directly from hunters on Lolland Island, in the Baltic Sea.

The waiter delivered a wooden tray of crunchy-chewy little bits of fried Jerusalem artichokes with horseradish cream and a glass of good Morgon. I covered a few slices of bread with some salty butter that had been whipped with little caramelized onions and found that I didn't feel stressed at all, either.

My friend the waiter returned to suggest today's chicken and named the farm it came from ("It's world-famous in Denmark," he said). It was meltingly tender and paired with roasted beets, slices of pickled pear, and beet leaves dressed in something buttery. I finished with a plate of Danish hay cheese with sticky dabs of green-walnut compote and watched the parade of bicycles riding by outside. Bicycles with buckets on the front for healthy groceries and happy children. Bicycles decorated and personalized and practical. Radio reminded me of those sensible Danish bicycles: an everyday thing that's well built but not showy, delivering what's asked of it, with a seat just for one.

It's a sign of how far things have come that it's taken for granted that even a neighborhood restaurant will have its own organic vegetable source, clean design, and good cheese. After lunch I walked over to Torvehallerne KBH, the city's covered food market. It isn't huge but its mere existence is a sign that interest in Nordic ingredients and cooking is making its way from high-level restaurants into the marketplace, changing how people shop and cook.

I carefully avoided eating anything more, and eventually headed to dinner at Geist, which faces Kongens Nytorv square. This is a more formal neighborhood, surrounded by palace gardens and the Royal Danish Theater. And Geist is of a different breed of restaurants than pretty much anything else in town. It was designed by Space, the same Copenhagen-based firm that put the woolly throws on the wooden chairbacks at Noma. Where that room is restful, Geist is revved-up. It feels like a flashy London restaurant, with none of the earthy, delicate qualities I'd come to expect in Copenhagen. It is a sleek and sexy machine in shades of swank grays and shiny black. The food, like the finishes, is stark and muscular.

A gigantic, L-shaped black bar seats 30 and surrounds a mostly black and shiny kitchen theater at the center of which Bo Bech performs nightly. The chef is, like that chicken, world-famous in Denmark. He looks as steely as his gleaming induction stoves, plating at a central station while around him an agile team of gray-smocked cooks pull an impressive range of things from sous vide baths, steam ovens, and simmering pots. The kitchen machine is, as Puglisi would say, hammering.

The food walks the line between sumptuous and brutalist, usually to good effect. Some of the dishes are monochrome: two gargantuan stalks of white asparagus dressed sparingly in a creamy white sauce on a black plate. Others are warming and direct: a rich potato purée with crabmeat, spooned up with a salty cloud of aerated butter; smoked eel with translucently thin shavings of cauliflower. Order a coffee and you get a big Einstein's-head of white cotton candy on the side.

Bech's cooking style seems rooted less in a Nordic culinary philosophy and more on a precise methodology: find great local ingredients, put a couple of them together in interesting pairings, cook them well, salt liberally, and get them onto the plate with a minimum of distracting fuss. Sit at the bar, order as many courses as you care to eat. It's modern restaurant cooking distilled to its elemental core. The food's not aim-for-the-fences ambitious or head-scratchingly brainy. It's engineered to please, and in that sense seems as timely as anything happening in the city.

One of the hallmarks of a city made for wandering is that the view is constantly changing, never dull. Copenhagen is Denmark's prettiest puzzle of islands and bridges, houseboat-lined canals and man-made urban lakes, twee red houses slumping into their ancient foundations and stately Rococo palaces. Walk long enough and you'll find yourself alone on a quiet canal, with only a seagull for company and an empty tugboat bearing the motto IT'S ONLY LOVE GIVE IT AWAY. Turn a few corners and here comes the Band of the Royal Danish Life Guards, stomping down the block in bibs and chin-strapped hats, banging their drums and blowing trumpets in the rain. (Come to think of it, I've never *not* seen a marching band in Copenhagen.)

It can be hard to see how the pieces fit together, different neighborhoods imprinting memories of distinct cities. Some places feel like different planets. One evening I walked to the address I'd written down for dinner and found myself facing the Danish national football stadium. The restaurant Geranium is affixed incongruously to the eighth floor of this arena, looking very much like it just crash-landed from Planet Fine Dining. All the cooks in the giant mission-control kitchen wear towering white toques. Their leader is Rasmus Kofoed, a chef who won the Bocuse d'Or competition, the "world cup" of chefs cooking things people don't actually eat. If this achievement happens to slip your mind, your waiter will certainly remind you when he invites you to visit Kofoed's gold, bronze, and silver trophies proudly displayed in the spotless kitchen.

What can I say about the food that emanated from this trophy room? It was flawless in its way. Precisely composed, good-tasting, lacking only a soul. There were

Lars "The Viking" Williams, head chef at the Nordic Food Lab.

no missteps, except that for me the entire enterprise felt misguided, empty. The actors knew their lines but the play was exquisitely boring. And the experience was hideously expensive. There is a menu called, without a wink, "our total universe tasting menu" (see, these betoqued visitors *have* crossed the universe!), which costs more than $500.

At the end of a very long meal, after we'd been treated to many explanations about the house specialties, after we'd been presented with the side of lamb bacon and lectured on the ways it would enhance a dish called

GUIDE

One of two food pavilions at Torvehallerne KBH. Right: A market stall selling just-picked carrots.

"herb garden," after we'd been shown the golden trophies and instructed to drink a glass of milk with one of the desserts, after we'd paid the staggering bill and were ready to leave this kitchen stadium—after all that, the waiter offered one last treat.

"Would you like to take a tour of our wine cave?"

"Not really, thank y—"

"Perfect, right this way..."

But the spaceship was the rigid, retrograde exception that proved Copenhagen's groovy rule. A few days later I returned to Noma for a visit to a very different vessel, where a more compelling form of culinary futurism is being practiced. The Nordic Food Lab is run out of a boat docked on a quay next to the restaurant. Redzepi helped found the independent institute in the summer of 2011. He introduced us to Lars Williams, a tall, tattooed, friendly American who heads up the kitchen for the lab. "If the Vikings still existed, they would look just like Lars," Redzepi said.

For the next hour or so Williams and Redzepi ran around the boat pulling out experiments in various stages of development for us to taste and smell. We sampled *garum*, that seasoning of the ancient Romans,

made from fermented herring. Aged yellow peas that had been turned into a kind of Scandinavian miso paste—pungent, delicious, and confusing. We sipped buckwheat fermented in the manner of sake. They've developed a seaweed cheese. All the lab's findings are made public in the hopes that big food companies will take up the task of using more of the edible landscape. Williams put a frozen canister into a Pacojet and whipped up seaweed ice cream.

"Fun stuff happens here," Redzepi said.

When or how all of this inventiveness will appear on restaurant menus or supermarket shelves, it's impossible to say. One thing Redzepi has accomplished that won't go away soon is to push fine dining away from an idea of stuffy luxury and nudge it toward his own style of lyric naturalism. There's an anti-fussy elegance to the new Nordic approach, and I hope it's catching.

I asked Redzepi why he sends the chefs out to introduce their dishes. "There is something important in that idea of putting two hands forward and saying: 'Here is something we made, we hope you like it.' The essence of a restaurant is a sensation of giving." +

europe

Paris

In a city with its share of culinary superlatives, the French pastry tops them all. Maybe it's the scent of freshly baked bread that fills the cobblestoned streets each morning or the sheer joy that comes from biting into a candy-colored *macaron*—the kind that have made Ladurée and Fauchon household names. But there are hundreds of lesser-known patisseries across Paris where the pickings are just as sweet. Here, our favorite places for a sugar rush.

Au Levain du Marais

Hidden on a quiet side street in the Bastille quarter, Au Levain du Marais has been a neighborhood mainstay for more than a century. Come before 9 a.m. for warm, buttery croissants and a steaming cup of café au lait, or try the flaky *chausson aux pommes*, puff-pastry triangles filled with warm apple compote. *28 Blvd. Beaumarchais, 11th Arr.; 33-1/48-05-17-14.*

Du Pain et des Idées

Fashion exec turned chef Christophe Vasseur traded in his Ferragamos for an apron more than a decade ago to run this *boulangerie* founded in 1875, in the Canal St.-Martin neighborhood. The menu runs the gamut: crackly baked loaves; spinach and goat-cheese pavés; aromatic butter brioche studded with orange blossoms. The highlight, however, is the nutty *pain des amis*, a thick-crusted flatbread that's fermented for two days before being cooked on stone in a wood-fired oven. *34 Rue Yves Toudic, 10th Arr.; 33-1/42-40-44-52; dupainetdesidees.com.*

Éric Kayser

A third-generation baker who has opened branches of his patisserie across the city, as well as in Moscow, Tokyo, and Manhattan, Éric Kayser excels at everything he creates, from crusty *baguettes de tradition* and apricot-pistachio tarts to such seasonal treats as the *bichon au citron,* a lemon-cream turnover sprinkled with sugar. *14 Rue Monge, Fifth Arr.; 33-1/44-07-17-81; maison-kayser.com.*

Gontran Cherrier

For a modern update on the iconic *boulangerie,* head to young chef Gontran Cherrier's brightly painted spot in Montmartre. Cherrier has made a name for himself by reinventing the classics, spicing up breads with unconventional ingredients such as bergamot, miso, and Sichuan peppercorns. Order a slice of the curry multigrain or chickpea-and-lemon loaf. *22 Rue Caulaincourt, 18th Arr.; 33-1/46-06-82-66; gontrancherrierboulanger.com.*

La Pâtisserie by Cyril Lignac

On a busy corner of Rue Paul Bert, across the street from his renowned bistro Le Chardenoux, spirited French television personality Cyril Lignac produces artfully designed traditional pastries, including *gianduja* éclairs (made with milk chocolate that's blended with dried fruits and almonds) and a raspberry tart piped with almond cream. *24 Rue Paul Bert, 11th Arr.; 33-1/43-48-19-50; lapatisseriebycyrillignac.com.*

Pain de Sucre

A mouthwatering diversion for shoppers in nearby Le Marais, the pint-size Pain de Sucre is owned by affable duo Didier Mathray and Nathalie Robert and known for its giant, airy marshmallows, which come in a range of flavors, from coconut to saffron. Another standout: the *pirouette pomme* (crunchy almond crust, pistachio and lime cream, and apples caramelized with rosemary). In the mood for something savory? Opt for the briny olive-tomato-and-anchovy turnover. *14 Rue Rambuteau, Third Arr.; 33-1/45-74-68-92; patisseriepaindesucre.com.*

Pâtisserie Boulangerie Blé Sucré

After stints at luxe hotels such as Le Bristol and the Plaza Athénée, Fabrice Le Bourdat opened the unassuming, though no less revered, Blé Sucré. His dainty, citrus-glazed madeleines are a sweet riff on the Proustian ideal, and his vanilla-mousse tart, crowned with sugar-dusted strawberries, is arguably the best in Paris. *7 Rue Antoine Vollon, 12th Arr.; 33-1/43-40-77-73.*

Pierre Hermé

The city's most creative assortment of *macarons* is still found at Pierre Hermé's chocolate-brown boutique on the Left Bank. Look for signature flavors such as rose and caramel and salted butter. Other crowd-pleasers: the *plaisir sucré,* a three-layer biscuit made with milk-chocolate wafers, hazelnuts, ganache, and chocolate chantilly; and the cheesecake topped with strawberries, rhubarb, and passion fruit. *185 Rue de Vaugirard, 15th Arr.; 33-1/47-83-89-96; pierreherme.com.*

BOULANGERIE 28

Desserts at Pain de Sucre. Left: Au Levain du Marais, in the Bastille quarter.

Fresh croissants at La Pâtisserie by Cyril Lignac. Right: Inside Du Pain et des Idées.

Pizza marinara con alici, a traditional Neapolitan pie with anchovies, at Pizzaria La Notizia, in Naples.

Antico Forno
Roscioli's house
specialty, topped
with sausage
and spinach.

Pizza Quest:
Napoli vs. Roma

BY ANYA VON BREMZEN / PHOTOGRAPHED BY ANDREA WYNER

izza is *sole nel piatto*—sun on the plate!" pronounces Enzo Coccia, quoting poetry at La Notizia, his Neapolitan pizza temple. But a bite of his pie topped with delicate clouds of *burrata* and fire-kissed Cetara anchovies and I'm murmuring "*ossigeno*"—oxygen. Coccia's ethereal *cornicione*, that crucial inch of raised crust, hosts a colony of irregular air bubbles, with a dough that smells tart, tastes sweet, and lands on our table puffy and undulating from its searing 60 seconds in an 860-degree oven. By pairing faster-burning beechwood with oak, Coccia explains, he coaxes different temperatures inside his domed model. Ah, yes. In the 21st century, poetry requires a touch of thermodynamics.

Enjoying a slice on the go outside Naples's Di Matteo.

Scientist, auteur, ur-traditional baker, Coccia belongs to a brilliant new breed of Italian *pizzaioli.* They talk of *Saccharomyces* (yeasts) and esoteric tomato varieties with aplomb, and even Italy's old-school bakers are starting to listen. Whether it's an austerely perfect marinara in Naples or a *pizza di patate* tickled with Tahitian vanilla in Rome, pizza is having an evolutionary moment under the Italian sun.

Few other dishes, of course, offer the intense, primal satisfaction of pizza—which explains why it flourishes globally not just as its own food group but as something more of an edible life force. Whether you're in São Paulo (bready pies topped, perhaps, with hearts of palm and linguiça sausage) or Singapore (anyone for pizza with chicken and kimchi at a Japanese-inspired chain?)

or on a New York corner past midnight scarfing down that iconic thin cheesy slice—pizza satisfies our collective craving for doughy crunch, char, and goo, with the bright kick of tomato. Pizza is the ideal street food: quick, convenient, cheap, filling. And its universal appeal brings as much curse as blessing, its Italian origins all but neglected, its rigorous architecture and form bastardized and abused. Global? How about galactic? More than a decade ago Pizza Hut delivered six-inch salami pies to astronauts at the International Space Station. In 2011, the Japanese wing of Domino's upped the ante by announcing plans to open a branch... on the moon. (It still hasn't happened.)

At this I said *basta.* America may be enjoying its own artisanal-pizza boom at this very moment, but having the right pie at the right place on its *Italian* home turf is like discovering pizza joy for the very first time. And so, craving to assess the work of visionary *pizzaioli* and to reexamine pizza's roots, my boyfriend, Barry, and I

Toppings for *pizza al taglio* at Rome's Pizzarium. Right: Pizzeria Gino Sorbillo, in Naples.

plotted a tour of the most exciting *pizzerie* of Naples and Rome, both new-wave and old-world. Which city wins the golden pizza paddle? Read on to find out.

NAPOLI!

A third-generation *pizzaiolo*, Coccia opened his original Pizzaria La Notizia in 1994 in the well-heeled Posillopo quarter. There he developed his ingenious method of a smidgen of yeast (an ounce will leaven more than a thousand *pizze*) and a 12-hour room-temperature fermentation, for airiness. The new La Notizia launched in 2010—same street but light years away. Futuristic temperature- and humidity-controlled fermentation chambers here reduce the margin of error to zero. "ZE-RO!" Coccia brags.

With its tomato-red chairs posed against an apple-green wall, the place is also a sleek shrine to Campanian products. Such as Fratelli Fusco dairy's pear-shaped Provolone del Monaco cheeses, aged in grottoes, or

Karma microbrewery's Lemon Ale with its intriguing hints of Sorrento citrus. On the backlit wine shelf sit inky reds from Terre del Principe, whose owners spearheaded the revival of the indigenous Pallagrello grape.

The crusts of La Notizia's three dozen *pizze* are elegant essays in smoke, air, and acidity, precisely matched to their toppings. Some are kneaded with the soft Caputo 00 flour; whole wheat is added for others. We try a spring still-life of favas, asparagus, and pungent Campanian pecorino from herb-fed Laticauda sheep. Then, a dusky-sweet pie of yellow tomatoes, green Cilento figs, and buffalo *bresaola*. On our seventh specimen—a whole-wheat calzone exploding with a bitter-chocolate lava—we realize something shocking. *We could eat even more.*

And we do—a lot more—the following day, venturing into the historic (and histrionic) Spaccanapoli district in the *centro storico*. One of the neighborhood's main arteries, the narrow Via dei Tribunali, resembles a long setup of crèches besieged by darting, beeping *motorinos*. Welcome to the home turf of traditional *pizza napolitana*. Gino Sorbillo *ciao*'s us at a marble table of his namesake pizzeria. Sorbillo, who is only 38, has a face from a Bronzino portrait, the kiss-kiss populist touch of a politico (in the past he's run in a mayoral primary), and rock-star status among Napoli's pizz-addicts.

"My *nonna* Carolina," he hoots. "Twenty-one children—all *pizzaioli!*"

Though he churns out 10 times more pies (1,000 every day) than Coccia, Sorbillo still delivers an exemplary crust: on the robust, chewy side, but artfully blistered and bubbly. Neapolitans will insist that *condimenti* (toppings) should never—ever!—detract from the *impasto* (crust). But Sorbillo's do. Behold the lyrical Mediterranean combo of shaved artichokes, Vesuvian Piennolo cherry tomatoes, aged goat cheese, and basil. Or the gutsy homage to the black Caserta pig, combining its *strutto* (lard) and salami with a salty, earthy, black-olive flourish. The classic margherita practically bursts with red, white, and green.

To comprehend the new Neapolitan *pizze*, you need your *pomodoro* Ph.D. Sorbillo opens some boutique cans for instruction. Here are the elongated, bright-tasting tomatoes from Agrigenus, a cooperative, he says, that is run by the head of the San Marzano DOP; there's a purplish, sugar-sweet specimen called *tigrato nero*. Cheese? Buffalo mozzarella is chichi, but the workaday cow's-milk *fior di latte* melts better. I'm told a Caserta dairy is now producing a unique cow-and-buffalo blend for Sorbillo's margherita.

Next, Sorbillo leads us off to his favorite nearby pizza parlors. At each we'll try the specialties *della casa*. Spaccanapoli *pizzerie* often double as *friggitorie* (fried-snack joints), and at the 1936 Di Matteo, up Tribunali, we're regaled with *pizza-fritta* magnificence. A giant golden-fried crescent, oozing ricotta and provola cheese dotted with *ciccioli* (cracklings), has me wondering how you can marry pizza-like chewiness with fritter-like fluffiness. A cult of Clinton has reigned here since the ex-prez famously stopped in for a bite in 1994. Other than Bill photos, Di Matteo is a well-lit neorealist dive with a thronged take-out counter and—it goes without saying—mementos of local soccer deity Diego Maradona.

Rome's Spanish Steps. Below: A tomato-and-cheese pizza with fresh basil at Pizzeria Gino Sorbillo.

Sorbillo requests a marinara to go. "Why is Neapolitan pizza wet in the center?" he asks Socratically. "Because...." He folds his pie in four like a handkerchief—*portafoglio* to locals—creating a self-saucing package. "Because Neapolitan pizza is street food," he declares. "Eaten on foot, on a bench."

Or on a *motorino?* Like the one with the munching maniac who almost runs over us outside.

We arrive unscathed at the nearby Il Pizzaiolo del Presidente, opened in 2000 by the late über-*pizzaiolo* Ernesto Cacialli. Beyond the visual fanfare of the ubiquitous Bill hangs a photo of Cacialli with chefs Heston Blumenthal and Ferran Adrià. This sends Sorbillo into scientific mode. "Yeast and its environment interact," he elucidates while we taste Presidente's pizza with smoked Agerola provola cheese, basil, and those Vesuvian vine-ripened *pomodorini.* I comment on the crust's remarkable suppleness.

"Each pizzeria is a unique microclimate," he goes on. "The same *pizzaiolo* will make a distinctly different crust a few yards away."

Enzo Cacialli, Ernesto's son, possessed of the round brow and stout neck of a legionnaire, adds his two bits in a thick Neapolitan dialect. "A great pizza?" he philosophizes: *"Amore. Passione. E sa-cri-fi-cio!"* I refrain from materialistically mentioning the Maserati of pizza ovens crafted by the most in-demand third-generation *forno* artisan Stefano Ferrara. Del Presidente, Sorbillo, and La Notizia are all proud owners of a Ferrara *forno,* with its gorgeous mosaic-tiled exterior and a refractive brick vault that can take 1,600-degree heat.

Bidding Sorbillo *arrivederci,* we hail a cab to an address secretly recommended by Coccia. It pulls up by Da Attilio, on a market lane resembling an Arab souk. The place doubles as a gem of a family trattoria, with Mamma cooking garlicky spaghetti with mussels and her son the *pizzaiolo* waiting tables. Just when I think no carb can surprise, here come porcini folded into a singed, tender, tubular *"pizza-cannolo."* And then wow! *Pizza alle carnevale*—shaped like a star, its stuffed points bursting with blobs of ricotta, its middle luscious with tomato sauce, mozzarella, and sausage. Fade out: syrupy *caffè* served in liqueur glasses, and Signora Maria Francesca's tall, not-too-sweet candied citrus cassata cake.

We board the train to Rome guzzling Ferrarelle fizzy water before the next onslaught of dough.

ROMA!

A pizza native to Rome? consider the *pizza al taglio:* baked in lengthy rectangles or oblongs, whacked into sections, weighed, and brusquely shoved across worn bakery counters. Under a glistening sheen of tomato sauce or shingled with rosemary-scented potato slices? Nice. But just as good *bianca* (no topping). Unlike the round Neapolitan "sun" blistered in wood-burning ovens, traditional *pizza al taglio* is baked in an iron *teglia* (pan), in a gas oven, provoking a different yeast biochemistry. Which is better? Tough call.

And then again there's pizza Bonci, from the eccentric thirtysomething iconoclast of Pizzarium.

> # Having the right pie at the right place on its *Italian* home turf is like discovering pizza joy for the very first time.

Gabriele Bonci, who trained as a chef and resembles a fidgety bear, likes to operatically kiss bread loaves and coo to his crusts—at least when TV crews are around. They often are. Bonci is famous for trolling villages for *lievito madre* (sourdough starter; his oldest is nearly 100 years old) and setting yeast traps up trees. Yeast—*wild* yeast—is the thing. Dismissing brewer's yeast as dead junk, Bonci has created a unique kind of *impasto:* neither Neapolitan bubbly, nor Roman chewy, but fluffy and bready and beautifully alive in the mouth. His dough embraces such esoteric flours as Kamut and enkir, from the organic Piedmontese mill Mulino Marino. Its almost liquid consistency—less flour equals fluffier crust—requires an ingenious pizza-shaping method, manipulations evocative of making fresh mozzarella.

When Pizzarium opened in 2003, customers balked at the subversive crust and chef-y toppings. Today global gastronauts throng into Bonci's dime-size joint in Trionfale, remodeled with modern slate.

A view over the
rooftops of
Naples and its
iconic bay.

Waiting on an order at La Gatta Mangiona. Right: Pizzaria La Notizia's state-of-the-art Uno Forno oven.

We're at Pizzarium ourselves, waiting for Bonci—and waiting, as usual. But time passes quickly when you're snagging piping hot squares topped with smoked ricotta and asparagus tips, then with pecorino, favas, and house-cured *guanciale*, then with tender nuggets of rabbit, grapes, and bitterish chicory. Not to overlook "LSD" (licorice, sausage, dates).

"So sorry! Gabriele...he not coming!" bleats an assistant. "*Un disastro!* He drop his *telefonino* in the oven!"

Cell phones aside, Bonci has spawned a movement in Rome. Next day we're at 00100, in hipster Testaccio. Named for Rome's former zip code—and the 00-type flour—this colorful cool-kid nook consists of a pair of marble half-counters and two benches outside under a graffitied wall. "Gabriele lends us his *lievito madre*," a server informs, handing us a slab of Bonciesque crust dressed with mozzarella and Stilton under drizzles of

port reduction. "The starter's from a Puglian village," he adds. "From *eleven* generations!"

Stefano Callegari, the owner, is giving the yeasty Bonci a run as Rome's pizza prince. He also co-owns the pizzeria Sforno—terrific but way out in the sticks—and Tonda, in the leafy suburb of Montesacro. Besides *pizza al taglio*, 00100 is famous for its genius *trapizzine: pizza bianca* triangles filled with saucy Roman stews that deliciously seep into the dough's porous crannies. Today there's tomatoey tripe, and tongue in sharp *salsa verde*—iconic Testaccio *quinto quarto* (offal). And *baccalà* cooked in a rich foil of onions, raisins, and pine nuts.

At this moment, Barry has an epiphany: everything tastes better on pizza.

We're still not done with Testaccio. Up along Piazza di Santa Maria Liberatrice, where *nonnas* promenade arm in arm and tattooed skateboarders threaten their peace, the classic pizzeria Da Remo awaits. If *pizza al taglio* is a lunchy snack, at night Romans dine on their own *tonda* (round) pizza variety. The crust? *Sottile* (thin) and *croccante* (crispy)—adjectives utterly reviled in Naples. Da Remo's wood-fired margherita is Twiggy to Napoli's Sophia Loren—wispy as a wafer with deliciously semi-burnt edges that crackle. Romans call this crust *scrocchiarella*. And they love it so much we wait almost an hour for our rickety sidewalk table—but who's complaining?

One-century-old *lievito madre*, eh? Eleven generations—eh, eh?" Giancarlo Casa is chuckling. Well, yes, even Bonci admits that at 100 years the dough starter destabilizes and needs the boost of much younger leavening.

Casa is no envious skeptic. Partners with Callegari at Sforno, he also owns the awesome La Gatta Mangiona ("eater-cat") in the residential Monteverde district, where kitty-themed artworks—by his father-in-law— hang above blue-checkered tablecloths. By 9 p.m. this pizzeria/trattoria is buzzing with youths in well-ironed T-shirts and ladies in big costume jewelry. To drink— a cult Baladin Almond 22 Faro beer? A minerally Slovenian white? The classic Roman pre-pizza fritters are exemplary here: pecorino-and-mint croquettes with tight, elegant breading; *suppli* (cheesy rice balls) updated with saffron and asparagus. Our verdant pizza—pesto, ricotta, zucchini—shows off a Napo-Romano crust: Neapolitan puffiness and crisp Roman edges—the best of both worlds. "The chaff in our Abruzzo bread flour," Casa says, "imparts a developed acidity." Ditto the 24-to-48-hour marathon fermentation. Who said yeast has to be from only grandmas or trees?

Belisssssimaaa!

A collective cheer goes up as our "pizza Igles" travels to table. Named for a famous Italian chef, Igles Corelli, it suggests the mythical *gargouillou* salad of French super-toque Michel Bras. Arranged on a base of baked candied tomatoes is a breathtaking bouquet of herbs, micro-lettuces, and edible petals—of pansies, forget-me-nots, and delicate garlic flowers. Pizza as framable art?

For *pizza bianca* as drug, we keep returning to Antico Forno Roscioli, off Campo dei Fiori. When I first got addicted to the crusty, salt-speckled stuff, the place resembled any other mom-and-pop bakery. Now it's gone spiffy with metal sculpture suspended over the sleek, dark marble counter. Using a natural yeast starter for his three-foot-long oblongs, master baker Pierluigi Roscioli also favors cool, long fermentation and a rest under an olive-oil glaze—to develop that upper-crust toastiness. The super-thin *rossa* shimmers with a red *pomodoro* sheen; pizza with basil and mozzarella clumps makes an ornamental herbal patch. But *bianca* is best.

Whack whack! go the blue-handled knives. No, no! regulars protest, wanting to wait for the next batch if the pizza has sat around for more than a nanosecond. This is anti-Neapolitan dough, crunch where you expect puff, resolving into a moist, profound chewiness that fills the mouth with something like the essence of pleasure. We buy our *bianca* and a garlicky slab of *porchetta* from the adjacent deli counter and eat our DIY panini under Campo dei Fiori's stern statue of Giordano Bruno, the priest/astronomer burned at the stake. Baking is science. And cosmology. In my dough delirium I'm pretty sure Giordano is nodding along. +

GUIDE

NAPLES
EAT
Da Attilio
*17 Via Pignasecca;
39-081/552-0479.* $$

Di Matteo
*94 Via dei Tribunali;
39-081/455-262.* $$

Il Pizzaiolo del Presidente
*120-121 Via dei Tribunali;
39-081/210-903.* $$

Pizzaria La Notizia
*94/A Via Michelangelo da
Caravaggio; 39-081/
1953-1937; enzococcia.it.* $$

Pizzeria Gino Sorbillo
*32 Via dei Tribunali; 39-081/
44-6643; sorbillo.it.* $$$

ROME
EAT
00100
*88-90 Via Giovanni Branca;
39-06/4341-9624;
00100pizza.com.* $

Antico Forno Roscioli
*34 Via dei Chiavari;
39-06/686-4045;
salumeriaroscioli.com.* $$

Da Remo
*44 Santa Maria della
Liberatrice;
39-06/574-6270.* $$

La Gatta Mangiona
*30-32 Via F. Ozanam;
39-06/534-6702;
lagattamangiona.com.* $$

Pizzarium
*43 Via della Meloria;
39-06/3974-5416.* $

Sforno
*110 Via Statilio Ottato;
39-06/7154-6118;
sforno.it.* $$

Tonda
*31 Via Valle Corteno;
39-06/818-0960;
tondatonda.com.* $$

Istanbul

Chefs across Istanbul are testing the boundaries of avant-garde cooking at a breakneck pace, but the food scene in the city's humble *esnaf lokantas* (lunch canteens) and *meyhane* (authentic taverns) remains traditionally steadfast. T+L reveals the best places to sample the tastes of old Constantinople—one bite at a time.

Aslan Restaurant

Gold merchants, antiques dealers, and leg-weary Grand Bazaar browsers feast on Turkish classics at Aslan Restaurant, near the Nuruosmaniye mosque. The rotating menu features comfort dishes such as Ottoman "lady's thighs" (fried meatballs made with minced beef and rice), spiced red lentil soup, and braised lamb shanks wrapped in eggplant. Pair them with a bottle of red from the domestically sourced wine list—many are impossible to find back home. *70 Vezirhan Cad., Fatih; 90-212/513-7610.* **$$**

Çiya Kebap Lahmacun and Çiya Sofrasi

Chef-ethnographer Musa Dağdeviren—who began cooking four decades ago at a kebab joint and now lectures about Turkish food internationally and has been profiled in the *New Yorker*—still threads Istanbul's best minced-meat skewers. They come laced with pistachios, grilled inside eggplants, or sauced with sour cherries. Other standouts, rediscovered from old folk recipes, include the sautéed *kaya koruğu* (bush greens grown in river silt) and fried *mumbar*—sheep intestine filled with rice and lamb. Next door, sister restaurant Çiya Sofrasi offers a heartier take on such staples, plus rich meat-and-vegetable stews. *43 Güneslibahce Sk., Kadiköy; 90-216/349-1919; ciya.com.tr.* **$$**

Kantin Lokanta

For nouveau riffs on age-old favorites, the skinny-jeans-and-status-sneakers brigade beats a path to Kantin Lokanta, in leafy Nisantasi. Chef Semsa Denizsel (a former food stylist) is the Alice Waters of Turkey, evangelical about everything local and seasonal. At her understated bistro, a small blackboard menu touts whatever's fresh: braised leeks, their natural sugar tempered by marinated green almonds; a diaphanous stew of favas, flat beans, artichokes, and grass-fed Thrakia lamb. Ask for a Turkish coffee at meal's end, served with aromatic mastic gum—an Ottoman-era palate cleanser. *30 Akkavak Sk., Nişantaşi; 90-212/219-3114; kantin.biz.* **$$**

Karaköy Lokantasi

In a gentrifying neighborhood by the docks near Galata Bridge, turquoise-tiled Karaköy Lokantasi is the *meyhane* of the moment. Owners Aylin Okutan and Oral Kurt keep their glass display stocked with some three dozen small plates—and that's just the cold appetizers. Order the lemony braised spinach roots, the smoked octopus, and the *börek* (a fried cheese-or meat-filled pastry), here loaded with shreds of aromatic *pastirma,* a cured beef. *37A Kemankeş Cad., Karaköy; 90-212/292-4455.* **$$**

Kiyi Restaurant

Eating fish along the Bosporus is a quintessential pastime in Istanbul. And natives maintain an almost irrational devotion to chef Yorgo Sabuncu's Kiyi Restaurant, where you can watch boats bob in the harbor from the second-floor terrace and the ritual is time hallowed. First: white tangy cheese, cubes of green melon, and raki. Next, the meze tray, with its obligatory iterations of eggplant and *lakerda,* a fatty, thick-cut, lightly cured Black Sea bonito. Then fish (turbot, anchovies, or perhaps sardines), prepared as simply as possible. *186 Haydar Aliyev Cad., Tarabya; 90-212/262-0002; kiyi.com.tr.* **$$$**

Münferit

The triple-distilled Beylerbeyi raki (made by owner Ferit Sarper's family) is as sought after as the Ottoman cuisine at Münferit, a contemporary haunt that draws a stylish crowd from Beyoğlu's main pedestrian thoroughfare. Courses of squid-ink couscous and mint-flecked fava-bean purée are served in the intimate dining room—or on the stone terrace—accompanied by crusty bread from Sarper's home village with anchovy butter. If you're looking for a quiet meal, this is not the place: a DJ spins loud tunes after 11 p.m. on weekends. *19 Yeni Carşi Cad., Beyoğlu; 90-212/252-5067; munferit.com.tr.* **$$**

Zarifi

Owner Fehmi Yaşar worked as a filmmaker before opening the cistern-like Zarifi, also in the Beyoğlu district. Yaşar specializes in traditional dishes from Istanbul's minority groups, including Sephardic Jews, Armenians, and Greeks. The honey eggplant has a pleasing sweet-savory flavor, and the *islim kebab*—lamb on the bone wrapped in lush eggplant—is a must-try. *13 Cukurlu Cesme Sk., Beyoğlu; 90-212/293-5480; zarifi.com.tr.* **$$$**

Visneli (meatball) kebab at Çiya Sofrasi, on the Asian side. Left: Aslan Restaurant's head chef, Adem Kiliç.

Fire-roasted anchovies on sourdough bread at Kantin Lokanta. Right: Karaköy Lokantasi's dining room.

Greek Wine
Country

BY BRUCE SCHOENFELD / PHOTOGRAPHED BY DAGMAR SCHWELLE

A plate of stewed snails by Maria Konstantaki at Crete's Boutari Wineries. Opposite: A church near Lyrarakis vineyards in Agios Vasileios, Crete.

The Peloponnesian port town of Nauplia. Left: *Dakos*, bread with tomato and feta, at Boutari Wineries.

George Skouras at his Domaine Skouras vineyards, in the Peloponnese. Right: Glasses of Nostos wine at Crete's Manousakis Winery.

might have fallen as hard for Plyto in a tasting room or over dinner at home, but the setting of our first encounter made it inevitable. I was on a sloop, sailing past the stone bastions of Spinalonga, the mysterious Venetian fortress off Crete's northern coast. Friends I'd met just that afternoon had laid out meats and cheeses beside canapés that looked like miniature sculptures. The sea was shimmering, the sky a shade of El Greco blue. Then came wine, from a grape variety I hadn't encountered in two decades of seeking out the stuff around the world. Not only did Plyto have historic importance—found solely on Crete, it was rescued from near extinction by a determined vine grower in

the 1980's—but its thirst-quenching, green-apple bite also made it the perfect beverage for a perfect moment.

But that's Greece. You can visit more famous wineries elsewhere, and drink bottles far more renowned (and certainly more expensive) while eating elaborate meals in your fanciest clothes, yet I've found few places where exploring wine regions is more fun. Almost everywhere I went during my two-week journey, I found panoramic vistas, intriguing wines, and hospitality on an Olympian scale. (Driving in Macedonia, I stopped for gas, walked inside to pay, and found a family of five eating homemade lentil soup that they insisted I sample.) It isn't all rustic tavernas and glorified pensiones, either. That sloop belonged to Elounda's Blue Palace, a sumptuous, 251-room hotel on a hillside overlooking Spinalonga that ranks for sheer magnificence with any place I've ever stayed.

You've heard that wine tastes better where it's produced, but that truism is especially valid in Greece. Greek food is famously simple: no elaborate postmodern constructions or complex sauces here. That leaves space for the wines to show themselves. And a palate needs steady exposure to get accustomed to the singular flavors of the country's grapes. At home, compared with Pinot Noirs and Cabernets, Greek wines can seem rustic, unsubtle, even strange. But calibrate your taste to their sturdy architecture and you'll start daydreaming about which to have with dinner.

America's boom in fine Greek restaurants has helped lift the profile of Greek wine. "We've been making it for four thousand years, but still hardly anyone knows it," lamented Yiannis Paraskevopoulos of Gaia Wines, which has wineries in the Peloponnese and on Santorini. But nobody needs to be sold on the charms of traveling in Greece. Though the financial crisis has cast a shroud over the tourism industry—and credit card machines, which create a record of a meal or hotel stay for tax purposes, seem to be "broken" at every turn—Greeks couldn't treat a visitor badly if they tried. Here are three regions that combine delicious food and surpassing natural beauty with memorable hotels, and wines that might even make you fall in love.

THE PELOPONNESE

Renaissance painters perceived Arcadia as a pastoral utopia. But as I gazed at jagged peaks and steep-walled valleys from the doorway of the tiny chapel in the Domaine Tselepos vineyard, or climbed a mountain road toward the Semeli winery's eight-room inn past yellow and purple wildflowers and imposing rock escarpments, this fabled region of the Peloponnese had a distinctly primordial cast. Though much of modern civilization evolved here, it seemed only a thin veneer.

The Peloponnese, a peninsula of more than 8,000 square miles that fills the southern third of mainland Greece, has a rich history that dates to ancient times.

The catch of the day at Nauplia's Savouras restaurant. Left: Flowers in bloom on a street in Nauplia.

Pan, the god of nature, is said to have sprung from the Arcadian forests. Sparta clashed with Athens on its plains, and Greek independence was fomented in its villages in the 1820's. So it's no accident that most of the grapes planted in the region are wholly and unabashedly Greek. "There are two approaches in Greece, international or indigenous varieties," Paraskevopoulos said. "Here in the Peloponnese, we chose the second one. The hard one."

In Mantineia, in the Arcadian hills near Tripoli, Moschofilero (mos-koe-*fee*-le-row) makes gorgeously transparent white wines. The best of them taste of the chilly summer nights that make the slow-ripening grapes among the last to be picked in all of Europe. Domaine Spiropoulos shares a plateau there with ancient ruins. An Athenian dentist started the winery on ancestral farmland in the 1980's, working weekends to inculcate his son, Apostolos, in the culture of growing grapes and making wine.

Apostolos Spiropoulos now runs the estate. He throws dinner parties in the flower-filled courtyard, guides tours of the organically certified vineyards, and

serves a bracing, unoaked version of Moschofilero that has the spine of a great Riesling. Taste it at the winery, then drink it by the bottle in the garden of the Taverna Klimataria Piteros, in Tripoli, alongside baked rooster, hand-cut pasta with a wisp of cinnamon, and bitter greens that coax sweet fruit out of the steel and flint.

In the valley below Mantineia sits Nemea, a red-grape region that extends almost to the edges of the port town of Nauplia (often spelled Nafplio or Nafplion). The dominant grape there, Agiorgitiko (ah-your-*yee*-ti-ko), can make a friendly but almost characterless wine that, in the wrong hands, is soft to the point of flabbiness. But the winemaker George Skouras does for that variety what *The Simpsons* did for cartoons, adding complexity without losing the spark that provides the fun. He started in 1986, applying lessons learned in enology school to the varieties of the region. Without realizing it, he'd joined a rising generation of winemakers around Greece who were attempting the same. "It became a movement," he said. "Almost a revolution."

Now Domaine Skouras makes some 700,000 bottles a year, while welcoming the waves of visitors who stop in

Locals outside the Church of Skalani. Left: Octopus, dolmas, and fava-bean spread at Crete's Blue Palace.

at its showpiece facility, a 90-minute drive from Athens. What they find is a range of wines that use precision rather than power to seduce. "We're a European winery, unabashedly," Skouras said. What he meant became clear when he poured me his Grande Cuvée, made from Agiorgitiko grown in volcanic soil. I was startled to learn that this wine—so composed, so well bred—can be found stateside for less than $29 a bottle. Later, at one of the many restaurants that ring the Nauplia harbor, I drank a Skouras rosé that looked pink and fruity like bubble gum, but smelled like fresh-cut flowers.

Nauplia resembles a less tidy version of St.-Tropez, without the glitter. It has a latticework of cobblestoned streets, a few hotels with aspirations and many more pensiones with colored shutters and earnest breakfasts, and enough good eating for a week's stay. I had my best meal there at Savouras, where customers are led to a vast wooden filing cabinet, the drawers of which are pulled open to reveal the day's catch on ice. Prices are far from cheap—my grilled snapper weighed in at $55—but the only fresher fish you'll find, I'm convinced, is on the boat that caught it.

MACEDONIA

Greek Macedonia isn't a country; that's the cumbersomely named (by UN decree) FYROM—former Yugoslav Republic of Macedonia—that borders it to the north. But geopolitics aside, perhaps it ought to be: this oblong region has the diversity of nations ten times its size. Fishing villages and beaches speckle the coastline; spits of land protrude into the Aegean like spiny fingers. Hilltop villages look out over forests roamed by chocolate-colored bears. Thessaloníki, Greece's second-largest city, climbs the hills that rise from its harbor like a denser, even stronger-flavored Genoa or Trieste, while the understated beach resorts around it cater to an international crowd. The food, architecture, and language of the region reflect centuries of influence by Turks, Serbs, and Bulgars.

"Our goal is to get the city to understand and be proud of its past," Yiannis Boutaris, Thessaloníki's mayor, told me when we met over coffee and whiskey at a local café. A newcomer to politics after a life in wine, Boutaris can be understood best as Greece's Robert Mondavi. Like Mondavi, he quarreled with his family,

A flower-filled
pedestrian alley
in Nauplia.

then left its industrial winery to compete against worldwide producers on quality, not volume. That's where the parallel ends. Ever the iconoclast, Boutaris ceded control of his wine business to his son in order to serve as the only big-city mayor I know of who has a tattoo of a lizard crawling up his hand.

Thessaloníki's forgotten past includes its connection to wine, which has been made nearby for centuries. Strolling its streets, reveling in the splendor of Greek and Roman ruins, Ottoman temples, and remnants of a once thriving Jewish presence, I encountered a jam of outdoor cafés, one pushed against the next, overflowing with men (and occasionally women) talking, playing cards or backgammon, and drinking coffee or ouzo, but rarely wine. As the hub of a wheel that leads to viticultural areas to the west, northwest, northeast, and south, the city is the ideal base for a tasting tour. Yet you'll find more accomplished Greek wine on tables in midtown Manhattan.

Outside Thessaloníki, that heritage becomes evident. An hour to the west is Naoussa, where Boutaris started his Kir-Yianni winery. Here the clay soils and mountain breezes, along with water so pure that nobody bothers to buy it bottled, create optimum growing conditions for Xinomavro (*zeeno*-mav-ro), Greece's most intriguing red grape. It's an antisocial variety that greets you with a rush of fruit, then turns its back and bares its fangs. Still, as made by Kir-Yianni or the tiny Karydas Estate, a winery in a house near where Aristotle purportedly once tutored Alexander, Xinomavro shows a crystalline depth that recalls Italy's Nebbiolo.

From there, I drove farther west and several hundred feet up to Amyndeo, the coolest wine region in Greece. In his zealously tended vineyards, Alpha Estate's Angelos Iatridis grows a painter's palette of varieties, from the indigenous Malagousia and Mavrodafne to Syrah, Pinot Noir, even Barbera. It's an intriguing blend of the local and the international, and so was the dinner we shared at Kontosoros, in the neighboring town of Xino Nero. Many Greek meals are basic affairs, which made Kontosoros a particular find. Meatballs with saffron; pork tenderloin beside frumenty pasta of wheat and yogurt; and a salad of wax beans, capers, pistachios, and scallions were composed with the artfulness—and imagination—that elsewhere

might earn chef Nikolaos Kontosoros a cooking show. It was the best meal I had in Greece.

The counterpoint to that ambitious food, and to the Alpine feel of Amyndeo and surrounding towns such as the delightful fairyland village of Nymfeo, was the fried mullet, grilled octopus, and other marine delights I devoured during my alfresco lunch at Agnandi. It overlooks the Aegean in Epanomi, south of Thessaloníki, in a setting of palm trees and striped awnings and rhythmic tides that could seem Caribbean. But the snap of fresh vegetables and the tang of feta is unmistakably Greek, and when it's clear, you can see Mount Olympus.

Nearby, down a rock-strewn dirt road that looks like the direct route to Nowhere, are the ivy-covered stucco walls of Domaine Gerovassiliou, the region's most attractive winery. The gardens are awash in color, the

Crete is a special place, where the distilled essence of Greece is augmented by African, Turkish, and other influences. For wine drinkers, the island is like Darwin's Galápagos.

museum features an epic corkscrew collection, and the wines are nothing if not polished. On the veranda, sipping a glass of white Malagousia that tasted of lemons and rosewater, I found it easy to forget that bottled wine in Greece (as opposed to wine poured for customers into flasks or jugs) is just a few decades old. Yet viticulture in Macedonia is also an ancient endeavor, and the same characteristics in the land and climate that enticed the original Greeks to cultivate grapes beside the olive trees are at work today. "We're starting to rebuild a tradition," Boutaris told me. "We're finding the special places that give special characteristics to the wines." Little by little, the world is noticing.

CRETE

If you visit only one destination in Greece, make it Crete. Sure, the trashy beach resorts and general decrepitude in and around Iráklion, the island's biggest city, have a decidedly Third World air. Driving is perilous, meals can be overpriced, weather frustratingly erratic. Even its barren mountains can seem inhospitable and menacing.

But persevere. Crete is a unique place, where the distilled essence of Greece is augmented by African, Turkish, and other influences. For wine drinkers, the island is like Darwin's Galápagos. The catalogue of grape varieties found mostly, or only, on Crete is more varied than that of anywhere I've been. If you have even a vague interest in wine, a few days on the island are sure to bring out your inner geek. If you're into it to begin with, well, it's like finding buried treasure.

That's how I felt when I tracked down Lyrarakis, the producer of that marvelous Plyto. I found the winery in the rural hills south of Iráklion, after my GPS had led me through a tangle of rutted roads. The winemaker met me bearing an armful of bottles, then went back for more, for Lyrarakis produces 17 different wines, none priced above $38. Soon I was immersed in a crash course in ampelography, the study and classification of grapevines. I tasted Vilana and Dafni, Vidiano and Kotsifali, Mandilari and Thrapsathiri—not one of

which, as far as I'm aware, has ever been commercially planted in the United States. Some, such as the massively structured Mandilari and the Plyto, were good enough that I schemed to ship a case home.

Nearby, past the famous Knossos ruins (which, sadly, have been "restored" to the extent that you can't tell whether a fresco is a 3,500-year-old original or a recent fabrication), is Boutari Wineries. The company owned by Yiannis Boutaris's family makes 2 million bottles a year of Moschofilero alone, yet its glass-walled Cretan facility (one of several in Greece) feels surprisingly intimate. The featured players on the day I visited were an evanescent white blend called Fantaxometocho, colloquially referred to as "ghost wine," and an impish middle-aged woman, Maria Konstantaki, who arrived from the kitchen bearing warm zucchini pie, bread with tomato and feta, and yogurt with sweet grapes. (Be forewarned: you'll need to make a reservation well in advance to sample her excellent cooking.) "Cuisine of the grandmother," she called it, then gave me a hug to show she meant it.

After two nights at the Blue Palace, I moved to Earino, a three-cottage hilltop inn renowned for its farm-fresh food. A chapel the size of a magazine

GUIDE

THE PELOPONNESE
STAY
Semeli
Koutsi, Nemea; 30-2746/020-360; semeliwines.gr. $

EAT
Savouras
79 Bouboulinas St., Nauplia; 30-2752/027-704. $$

Taverna Klimataria Piteros
11 Kalavriton St., Tripoli; 30-271/022-2058; taverna-sideris.gr. $$

TASTE
Domaine Skouras
Malandreni; 30-2751/023-688; skouraswines.com.

Domaine Spiropoulos
Mantineia; 30-2796/061-400; domainspiropoulos.com.

Domaine Tselepos
Rizes; 30-2710/544-440; tselepos.gr.

Gaia Wines
Nemea; 30-2108/055-6423; gaia-wines.gr.

MACEDONIA
STAY
Palea Poli
Naoussa; 30-2332/052-520; paleapoli.gr. $

EAT
Agnandi
Epanomi Beach, Thessaloníki; 30-2392/041-209. $$

Kontosoros
Xino Nero; 30-2386/081-256; kontosoros.gr. $$

TASTE
Alpha Estate
Amyndeo; 30-2386/020-111; alpha-estate.com.

Domaine Gerovassiliou
Epanomi, Thessaloníki; 30-2392/044-567; gerovassiliou.gr.

Domaine Karydas
Naoussa; 30-2332/028-638; diamondwineimporters.com.

Kir-Yianni
Naoussa; 30-2332/051-100; kiryianni.gr.

CRETE
STAY
Blue Palace
Elounda; 30-2841/065-500; bluepalace.gr. $$$

Casa Delfino
Canea; 30-2821/087-400; casadelfino.com. $$

Earino Kato
Asites, Iráklion; 30-2810/861-528; earino.gr. $

TASTE
Boutari Wineries
Skalani; 30-2810/731-617; boutari.gr. $

Lyrarakis
Alagni; 30-2810/284-614; lyrarakis.com.

Manousakis Winery
Canea; 30-2821/078-787; nostoswines.com.

kiosk sits on the property, and one morning of my
visit coincided with the only religious service held
there each year, on the anniversary of the death of the
proprietor's mother. When I heard bells, I stepped
outside my room to see villagers seated in metal chairs
positioned around the courtyard. They were dressed
in hand-sewn clothes of bright blue and white, the same
hues as the sky above and the cottages around us.
It might have been a hundred years ago, or a thousand.

A day later, in Canea, or Chania—a small coastal
city of warrens and passages, blind alleys, souvenir
shops, and restaurants serving provocatively
traditional dishes such as spiced rabbit with escargot—
I walked along a seawall to a lighthouse that had been
built by the Egyptians. I checked in to Casa Delfino,
a 17th-century Venetian mansion with a spa, an
authentic Turkish hammam, 500-year-old stones, and
a roof terrace. Then I drove into the hills to see the
Manousakis Winery.

The scene was almost comically rustic. Picture an
unsteady table in a backyard, flies buzzing, roosters
crowing, apricots and lemons swaying drowsily from

trees. Except that pouring me a glass of their Nostos
wine was Alexandra Manousakis, a pretty 29-year-old
from Washington, D.C., whose father, Ted, owns the
Bread and Chocolate chain there. *Nostos*, it turns out,
means nostalgia, which is what Ted, who left Crete
for America at 11, felt keenly whenever he returned to
visit. So he started a winery, and Alex, an NYU grad
who had previously worked for a New York marketing
firm, agreed to tend it.

Instead of local varieties, Ted planted the grapes
of the Rhône. "My father wasn't living here, so he
had no loyalties to Greek grapes," Alex told me. Nostos's
blend of Syrah, Mourvèdre, and Grenache, typically
found in Châteauneuf-du-Pape, rumbled with
dark earthiness, and the varietal Syrah showed all the
requisite blue and black fruit.

Each time I took a sip, a rooster crowed. A few
years before, newly relocated from Manhattan,
Alex might have been startled. Now she just smiled
and lifted an eyebrow, as if such a thing happened
all the time on this magical island. Maybe it does.
I wouldn't be surprised. ✦

europe

135

A sampling of Moroccan salads and *harissa* at a stall in Marrakesh's Djemaa el-Fna square.

Africa + The Middle East

South Africa, by the Roots

BY DOUGLAS ROGERS / PHOTOGRAPHED BY DOOK

A private deck and pool at Delaire Graff Lodges & Spa. Opposite: Updating the daily menu at Babel, a restaurant in Babylonstoren.

Le Quartier Français. Right: Poached crayfish at Reuben's Restaurant & Bar.

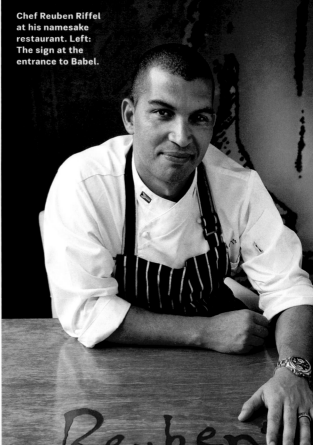

Chef Reuben Riffel at his namesake restaurant. Left: The sign at the entrance to Babel.

Consider, if you will, the vegetable garden. Every Afrikaner farm worth its salt has one—a testament to the white African tribe's almost mythic love for the land—and there's no reason why Babylonstoren, a handsome, 1692-built Cape Dutch homestead turned luxury hotel and working guest farm in the Franschhoek Valley of the Cape Winelands, should be any different. But this garden is on an altogether grander scale. I'm sitting in the sleek kitchen of my suite, a modern glass cube attached to a traditional thatched-roof, 18th-century *landhuisie* (cottage), and I'm gazing out on eight acres of organic wonder: scented beds of thyme,

rosemary, and garlic; blocks with Cape gooseberries and mulberries; a pergola walk dripping with table grapes; an orchard of *naartjies*, nectarines, and grapefruit watered by a restored sluice system; even an apiary for honey. And vegetables, too—butternut and beets; rocket and radishes; peppers of impossibly bright hue. If it all looks meticulously landscaped, it is—by French designer Patrice Taravella, creator of the medieval monastery gardens at Prieuré Notre-Dame d'Orsan, in the Loire Valley. In the distance, clouds tumble over craggy peaks and vineyards stretch to emerald foothills, but it's the garden that has me enchanted.

Best of all, it's mine. In the ultimate farm-to-table fantasy, as a guest I get to walk its mazy paths, pick whatever herbs, fruits, and vegetables I fancy—there are some 300 edible varieties—and prepare them in my designer kitchen. And if I don't fancy cooking? Well, I can just amble down a tractor-cut road outside my door to Babel, one of the farm's two restaurants. A milk-white, cement-floor room, it has a daily menu written on a tiled wall dominated by a giant print of a bull's head—a pricey piece bought in Milan by Babylonstoren's co-owner and designer Karen Roos. Why a bull? Well, this space used to be the cattle kraal, of course.

Twenty years ago, Franschhoek—Afrikaans for "French corner," named for Huguenot refugees granted land here in the 1680's—was a somnolent farming backwater. In the mid 1990's, as South Africa emerged

from the isolation of apartheid, trendsetting pioneers arrived to open inns, wineries, and restaurants. A decade later, the valley had been transformed into an African Provence (in a Switzerland-like setting), a hub for great food and wine and stylish living. Its top properties, Le Quartier Français and La Residence, and restaurants and wineries, such as Reuben's Restaurant & Bar, became destinations in their own right. Since then, a slate of glamorous hotels and restaurants, with Babylonstoren at the forefront, have been upping the ante, embracing a confident new South African style that reflects the region's past as much as its future.

Only a few years ago, the idea that a chic South African hotel could be a celebration of Afrikaner style and culture—let alone farm living—would have been unthinkable. But a generation since the end of apartheid, liberated from the guilt of the past, a wave of creative Afrikaners are forging a fresh identity. Afrikaans musicians are all over South Africa's airwaves and beyond, and Afrikaans authors far outsell their English counterparts. Babylonstoren is the design equivalent of this cultural resurgence.

"When apartheid was at its most stolid, it was *yech* to be Afrikaans," says Roos, an iconic fiftysomething former fashion magazine editor. "Now with moral respectability has come a certain coolness."

Roos and her husband, Koos Bekker, a multimillionaire Afrikaner media mogul, both grew up on farms and (as busy businesspeople often do) wanted a rural retreat. They bought the 590-acre property—one of the oldest and best-preserved Cape Dutch–style estates—in 2007 and opened it to guests in 2010. "One endearing trait about Afrikaners is a genuine love of the land," Roos says. "Culturally, the idea of heaven for us has always been a piece of land of our own, even if it means having to scratch to make a living."

What Roos has done at Babylonstoren is merge its authentic, no-frills earthiness with contemporary design to create a sort of "haute Afrikaner" style. Take the check-in area opposite the restaurant. No farmer would require his guests to "sign in," so the reception is modeled instead on a traditional farm store. There are computers here, but they sit on weathered tables hidden behind artfully placed mounds of fresh-picked beets and lettuce; there are shelves with mud boots and sun

Only a few years ago, the idea of a hotel celebrating Afrikaner style and culture would have been unthinkable.

hats for sale, but these boots have designer labels, and the hats are stylish fedoras. This playful embracing and defying of tradition continues outside. You won't find a shimmering blue swimming pool on the property—what farm has that?—so guests cool off in the property's reservoir, which is lined with chic lounge chairs. Nothing has been left to chance.

Beside the gabled manor house, accommodations are in 14 stand-alone *landhuisies*—all missionary-white stucco, set under the shade of oak and wild olive trees. The interiors, with their white sofas and rugs, Victorian tubs, and four-poster beds, manage to combine the austerity of a traditional Boer farmstead with the cool minimalism of Philippe Starck. Even here, authenticity rules: each cottage has a library of some 50 books handpicked by Bekker, most in Afrikaans.

The garden, though, remains the centerpiece. Roos gave Taravella license to re-create the geometry of the original Dutch East India Company's Garden,

established at the Cape in 1652 to supply fresh produce to their ships sailing between Europe and the Spice Route—the reason for the first Dutch landing at the Cape. To the formal rectangular layout of the garden with its 14 distinct blocks Taravella added his own flourishes: that avenue of dripping grapevines, pollination plants for the apiary, a lotus pond, and a series of pyramid-shaped towers draped in roses. If the history of the Afrikaner people can be traced back to the planting of a single garden, this is a glorious contemporary tribute.

Less than 10 miles from Babylonstoren, another tribute to Afrikaner heritage has gone up, this one at La Motte, a 420-acre wine estate owned by opera singer Hanneli Rupert-Koegelenberg. The sister of Johann Rupert, billionaire executive chairman of Swiss-based luxury goods company Richemont (owner of Cartier, Piaget, Chloé, and other brands), Rupert-Koegelenberg is effectively Afrikaner royalty. The family owns three wine estates in the valley, one in partnership with the Rothschilds, but La Motte has the most interesting aesthetic, especially since Rupert-Koegelenberg unveiled a museum and restaurant on it.

Set in rolling foothills near Franschhoek village, the estate's approach is memorable for its 13-foot-tall bronze sculpture of a woman bearing an overflowing glass of wine; rising out of the vines, against a sheer mountain backdrop, it's a dramatic sight. The museum and restaurant, surrounded by lawns and giant oaks, are both dedicated to South African master painter Jacob H. Pierneef, who was of Dutch and Afrikaner descent. Revered in his 1930's heyday, Pierneef's monumental South African landscapes—formal, flat, drained of color—had faded from fashion over the years. But in keeping with the current Afrikaner vogue, his work is poised to make a comeback. With fine timing, Rupert-Koegelenberg purchased 44 of Pierneef's paintings for display in a glass-walled museum that faces the lawn.

Pierneef is also the inspiration for the estate's restaurant, Pierneef à La Motte, a sprawling space in muted green and cream tones that recall his dramatic landscapes. The menus and high-backed chairs are all embossed with portraits of Pierneef and his daughter. Giant chandeliers made from replicas of Dutch East India Company–era porcelain hang from barnlike

Setting tables
in the garden
area at Pierneef
à La Motte.

A team of ducks near Babylonstoren's vegetable garden.

ceiling beams. The vintage plates, cups, and saucers chime like church bells when a breeze blows through.

In a state-of-the-art open-plan kitchen, chef Chris Erasmus executes modern twists on traditional *Boerekos*—Boer food that dates back 350 years. Indeed, just as Taravella was inspired by the Company's Garden, Erasmus spent months sifting through settlers' diaries, cookbooks, letters, and manuscripts, finding original recipes and ingredients that had been lost over time. The result is extraordinary: a menu that's a culinary archive of a people. A saffron fish curry recalls the food of the Malay slaves shipped to the Cape; a Huguenot fish pie was a favorite of those 17th-century refugees; and meaty dishes such as pomegranate-glazed pork belly and braised veal knuckle reflect the Dutch, German, and Flemish roots of Afrikaner food. "You can't eat history, but you can be inspired by it," Erasmus says.

At around the same time Babylonstoren and La Motte were opening, another property was unveiled in the area: Delaire Graff Lodges & Spa, a 100-acre estate located on the crest of Helshoogte Pass, a soaring mountain traverse that links Franschhoek with the more commercial wine and farming region of Stellenbosch. At first glance, the estate seems like a cosmopolitan mash-up. Billionaire British diamond jeweler and art collector Laurence Graff bought the estate in 2003 and spent six years building Delaire, hiring celebrated London designer David Collins to do the interiors. There are 10 lodge suites on the western flank of the property, each with an infinity plunge pool and a timber deck overlooking the Winelands. Stunning though they are, there's nothing particularly South African about the suites' aesthetic. Indeed, the estate's Indochine restaurant indicates a certain Eastern sensibility at work.

But at its heart, the property is as grounded in the Winelands as those earthy Afrikaner properties in the valley below. The main restaurant-winery, at the end of the long, oak-shaded drive, has giant wooden doors that swing open onto a soaring reception area backed by the glass walls of a winery holding two floors of stainless-steel vats and oak barrels. Underfoot is a smooth, dimpled floor made of peach pips and red resin—a contemporary take on the peach-pip, cow-dung, and oxblood floors once used in Cape Afrikaner homes. The restaurant has swanky orange banquettes that recall a New York City supper club, but the walls are lined with paintings by South African artists,

Washing radishes at Babylonstoren.
Left: The entrance to Waterford Estate.

among them a stunning William Kentridge portrait that's as imposing as that bull at Babylonstoren.

The menu combines modern with traditional as well: a quail with zucchini and sun-dried olives has been roasted, old Cape style, in a wood-fired oven, and grilled antelope loin is paired with winter vegetables and poached Natal plum, a tart fruit that tastes like

a cranberry. When I ask where my quail comes from, I'm directed to a farm in the valley; the oysters and mussels were harvested from Cape waters. As for the vegetables, they are very local: from Delaire Graff's own garden. These days, it's not just self-respecting Afrikaner farms that need vegetable patches. It seems any new property in the Winelands requires one. ✦

GUIDE

STAY

Babylonstoren
R45 near Simondium, Franschhoek; 27-21/863-3852; babylonstoren.com. **$$$$**

Delaire Graff Lodges & Spa
Helshoogte Pass, Stellenbosch; 27-21/885-8160; delaire.co.za. **$$$$$**

La Residence
Elandskloof Private Rd., Franschhoek; 27-15/793-3977; laresidence.co.za. **$$$**

Le Quartier Français
16 Huguenot Rd., Franschhoek; 27-21/876-2151; lqf.co.za. **$$$**

EAT

Pierneef à La Motte
La Motte Wine Estate, R45, Franschhoekweg, Franschhoek; 27-21/876-8800; la-motte.com. **$$**

Reuben's Restaurant & Bar
19 Huguenot Rd., Franschhoek; 27-21/876-3772; reubens.co.za. **$$**

TASTE

Ernie Els Wines
Annandale Rd., Stellenbosch; 27-21/881-3588; ernieelswines.com.

Haskell Vineyards
Annandale Rd., Stellenbosch; 27-21/881-3895; haskellvineyards.com.

Haut Espoir
Excelsior Rd., Franschhoek; 27-21/876-4000; hautespoir.com.

Thelema Mountain Vineyards
Helshoogte Pass, R310, Stellenbosch; 27-21/885-1924; thelema.co.za.

Villiera Wines
Corner of Old Paarl Rd. and Klipheuwel Rd., Stellenbosch; 27-21/865-2002; villiera.com.

Waterford Estate
Blaauwklippen Rd., Stellenbosch; 27-21/880-5300; waterfordestate.co.za.

Welbedacht Wine Estate– Schalk Burger & Sons
Oakdene Rd., Wellington; 27-21/873-1877; schalkburgerandsons.co.za.

Marrakesh

Whether in the souks of the walled medina or the bourgeois district of Guéliz, there is no better place to savor the diversity of North African cuisine than this ancient city's crossroads. For authentic lamb, couscous, eggplant—all redolent of cumin, saffron, and peppery *harissa*—don't miss one of these local favorites.

Al Baraka

The meal of your life...at a gas station? Indeed. A hop along the old Fez route brings you to Al Baraka, its cheery outdoor tables an agreeable distance from the pumps. Here's the drill: flatbread—as blistered and chewy as Rome's best *pizza bianca*—from a window where Berber ladies slap dough into a wood-fueled oven. Next, grilled lamb from the butcher shop in the middle. Finish with a tender beef shank fragrant with cloves and sweet, smoky prunes at the *tagine* station. *RP 24 Commune Annakhil, Sidi Yousef Ben Ali; no phone.* **$$**

Al Fassia Aguedal

Run by the female members of the Chab family, Al Fassia Aguedal is equally adored by tourists, opinionated French expats, and Marrakesh foodies. Bilingual servers walk you through the 15 small plates: three sumptuous iterations of carrots, an orange-blossom-scented tomato jam, and dainty, crisp *briouat* pastries.

9 bis Rte. de l'Ourika, Zone Touristique de l'Aguedal; 212-524/381-138; alfassia.com. **$$$**

Al Jawda and Al Jawda Plus

"Artistique!" cry sweet-toothed natives about the sugary *ghriba* cookies at Madam Alami's Al Jawda pastry shop. For something more savory, claim a chair on the terrace of Al Jawda Plus, her Parisian-looking tearoom, and order the definitive version of *pastilla*, Morocco's baroque pigeon pie. Crunchy yet light without the usual excess dusting of sugar, the pastry encloses a marvel of chunky braised pigeon, ground almonds, and beaten eggs. *11 Rue de la Liberté, Guéliz; 212-524/433-897.* **$**

Dar Moha

This restaurant bills itself as *nouvelle marocaine*, but its celebrity chef-owner Moha Fedal happily takes an *ancien* approach to couscous. Start with a mosaic of Moroccan salads at your candlelit table on the poolside patio of French designer Pierre Balmain's former *riad*. Midway through dinner, a duo of couscous dishes invites you to compare earthier Berber-style barley pellets with the more familiar durum wheat, here as light and fluffy as snowflakes. *81 Rue Dar el Bacha, Medina; 212-524/386-264; darmoha.com.* **$$$**

Espace Fruits Outmane

A cult morning classic, Espace Fruits Outmane might be miniature, but it's mirrored, tiled, and festooned with soccer-ball-scale papayas and grapefruits. While awaiting your omelette with dusky shreds of *khelea* (dried preserved beef) at the rickety plastic tables outside, slather aromatic flat cornbreads with honey and *amlou*, a rich almond-and-argan-oil spread that will ruin peanut butter for you forever. *40 Ave. Moulay Rachid, Guéliz; no phone.* **$**

Haj Mostapha and Chez Lamine

By day, local *mechoui* (roasted lamb) emperor Haj Mostapha N'Guyer presides over his Haj Mostapha stand in the medina in robe and skullcap. But at Chez Lamine, in upscale Guéliz, you'll find him each evening speaking French and sporting a European-style suit. The lamb at both locations is spectacular, roasted in an underground clay pit until meltingly tender, sold by the kilo, and served on butcher paper with cumin salt. *Souk Quessabine, off the northeastern end of Djemaa el-Fna; no phone.* **$** *19 Angle Ibn Aicha and Mohamed El Beqal, Résidence Yasmine, Guéliz; 212-524/431-164.* **$**

La Grande Table Marocaine

The cliché "royal repast" reacquires its zing at the extravagant Royal Mansour Marrakech hotel, owned by the king of Morocco. Here, Parisian chef Yannick Alléno oversees a trio of restaurants, including La Grande Table Marocaine, where the city's bon vivants dine beneath chandeliers that glitter onto filigreed metal tables. The highlight: *seffa medfouna,* a complex quail-and-raisin stew, buried in a mound of thrice-steamed vermicelli ornamented with almonds and cinnamon. *Rue Abou Abbas el Sebti, Medina; 212-529/808-080; royalmansour.com.* **$$$$**

Plats Haj Boujema

Once a popular hole-in-the-wall, Plats Haj Boujema retains its cheap prices and populist spirit despite its (almost) spiffy newer digs in Guéliz. Succulent minced lamb *kofte* precede perfect beef brochettes, then flash-charred lamb chops and, for the adventurous, skewers of plush liver or brains. No tasting is complete without the eggplant-and-tomato relish. *65 Mohamed El Beqal, Guéliz; 212-524/421-862.* **$**

Couscous with seven vegetables at Dar Moha. Left: Delivering a *tagine* at Al Baraka.

Royal Mansour Marrakech hotel's La Grande Table Marocaine restaurant. Right: Mint tea at Haj Mostapha.

Diners feast on chef Ali Hussain's Lebanese meze at Al Nafoorah, at the Jumeirah Emirates Towers.

Eating Dubai

BY GARY SHTEYNGART
PHOTOGRAPHED BY BAERBEL SCHMIDT

"Do you have the code?" It is a ninety-five-degree October day in Dubai. I am standing on the back lawn of the world's tallest building, the Burj Khalifa, the one scaled by Tom Cruise in the latest of his *Mission: Not Possible* movies, facing a dapper African security guard. But, unlike Mr. Cruise, I do not have the code. What I have is heatstroke. The Kenyan sentry appraises the melting man before him. "Oh, no, sir, I can't let you in," he says. "You have to be dressy. You have to be," he takes his time, relishing the word: *"eh-le-gant."*

Chastened, I shuffle off to the circular drive filled with Ferraris and Maseratis that separates the world's tallest tower from the world's biggest mall. FASHION: IMPOSSIBLE announces a giant Bloomingdale's poster. The mall gives on to a man-made creek that leads to a fake souk that turns back into a real mall, then twists into a garage and then circles back to become a mall again. Oblivious to the heat, a gaggle of ex-U.S.S.R. girls are sitting on the souk/mall's restaurant patio smoking *shisha* pipes. A woman in a black niqab shovels biryani past her veil, while her uncovered daughter makes quick work of an iPad. I stare at the glistening top of the world's tallest building, which looks like a beautiful steel flower reaching out to the desert skies. Before being stopped by security, I had been trying to get to the At.mosphere restaurant, the world's highest. All I wanted was some lunch.

"The Confirmation Code Has Been Sent to Your Room, Sir"

Now we're getting somewhere. I thank the concierge and hang up my bedside phone, which is about the size of my first 1980's Apple computer. I'm staying in the Jumeirah Emirates Towers hotel, one of the twin Emirates towers, which look like crisp space-age steam irons against the busy Dubai skyline. Gazing out my window, I see an ocher construction site resembling a fresh Zuni fortification. Beyond it, somewhere in the haze, is a coastline. I dash to the shower, put on my blazer, and wait for the code to be slipped under the door. Success! I read it aloud in case an unlikely wind sweeps off the Persian Gulf and deposits it in the lunar dust of another construction site. A4DEl, A4DEl, A4DEl.

An hour later, my taxi is stuck on the multilane insanity known as Sheikh Zayed Road, Dubai's principal thoroughfare. Unless I tell you otherwise, I am writing every word of this while stuck in traffic, lost between dozens of reflective green skyscrapers, with the Indian cabdriver blasting Virgin Radio FM, usually "Like a G6" by Far East Movement, or some other song about expensive planes, trains, and helicopters.

To ascend to the world's highest restaurant in the world's tallest building, one goes through the Armani Hotel. After I present my credentials at reception, an elegant Chinese woman with a British accent takes

The view from At.mosphere, on the 122nd floor of the Burj Khalifa.

me through the stylishly morose lobby to an elevator that takes us down to a second lobby, where I am handed over to a statuesque Russian. Many key cards are swiped along the way, into elevators, into turnstiles. And then, finally, I am zooming up at 33 feet per second into the future, as my ears pop and pop some more.

Gentlemen Are Expected to Spend at Least 200 Dirhams

I'm not sure if Dubai has its own anthem or coat of arms, but if it does it should definitely include the words MINIMUM SPENDING FOR GENTLEMEN IS AED 200. This is the sign that greets me at the entrance to the At.mosphere Lounge and will follow me around my week in Dubai. At this point, I am ready to eat my 200 dirhams (about $50). Instead, I am offered afternoon tea. The highest high tea in the world, natch.

I have ascended into the bosom of female Dubai expat society, surrounded by Marina Marys and Jumeirah Janes, those wonderful British ladies in flowery dresses who keep the local real-estate market from plummeting into the Arabian Gulf. In the pleasant circular room, I nibble on truffle-and-egg sandwiches and drink down my Laurent-Perrier Brut as the harpist

Pan-fried ortolan and pickled vegetables at Al Nafoorah. Left: A waiter outside Ravi Restaurant.

serenades us. Outside the 122nd-floor window: Dubai.

The sun sets bleakly over the sail-like extravagance of the Burj Al Arab, the exceedingly luxurious hotel moored on an artificial island to the north. Closer by, the faces of the ruling sheikhs of the United Arab Emirates drape a small skyscraper, a strange reminder that there are actually people in the country, citizens, I suppose, who are not Indian or Pakistani or Russian or British or German. A thousand airplane warning lights are blinking off a thousand skyscrapers as the sun sets. Gigantic cooling fans are spinning within the incomplete ruins of half-finished buildings. Beyond them a cartography of growing desire: malls, housing estates, artificial lagoons, the endless lunar sands of further construction. A Russian-accented Asian woman named Valeria, surely from one of the Stans, deposits a tray of *macarons* before me. If you could hear the traffic below it would sound something like Henderson the Rain King's "I want, I want, I want."

I Want a Drink

I've come to Dubai to write a story about food. My friend, the lovely Nouf Al-Qasimi, has joined me on this mission. She is a Yale-educated, Santa Fe–based foodie whose family lives in a gracious, jasmine-scented compound in Abu Dhabi. As with many Abu Dhabians, Nouf's view of Dubai, the brasher, far more outrageous emirate, can be summarized with an arched eyebrow.

I meet up with Nouf at the bar and restaurant Teatro, in the Towers Rotana Hotel Dubai, another heap of reflective blue glass on Sheikh Zayed Road. Nouf wants to introduce me to Pat, the Indian manager of Teatro, who seems to know all of Dubai, from the highest rulers to the lowest punters. Teatro's bar, a standard-looking rectangle lost beneath a healthy cloud of old-fashioned smoke, is where Dubai's populace feels most comfortable. We're listening to an instrumental version of "Like a Virgin" beneath portraits of Clark Gable. Pat examines my list of Dubai eateries: "No. Bad. Awful. No soul. Okay." I cheerfully cross off the offending places. "The thing about Dubai," Pat says, "is it's all steel and chrome—the heart is elusive."

We are joined by Nader Sobhan, an old classmate of Nouf's at Yale. Born in Rome to Bangladeshi parents and speaking perfect American English, Nader is the consummate Dubai resident: a son of three countries who lives in exactly none of them. I am immediately pleased by his short stature and hirsuteness, traits that

I happily share. Nader's full name means "rare glory," and he foresees our evening very clearly. Tonight we will skip the towers of the center, the "steel and chrome," to quote Pat, and head across the Dubai Creek for a glimpse of something real. And so, along with Nader and his Chinese girlfriend, we cram into a taxi and leave behind the heroic skyscrapers and well-groomed malls for a land called Deira.

With its 1980's architecture in disrepair, Deira reminds me of the New York borough of Queens on an especially humid day. There are Cyrillic signs everywhere advertising MEX, or "fur" in Russian. Our first stop is the Japanese restaurant Kisaku, up on the top floor of the disheveled Al Khaleej Palace Hotel. The quotient of actual Japanese salarymen is high here, the décor is minimal, the food is authentic and superb and although gentlemen will probably spend more than 200 dirhams, there are no signs commanding them to do so.

There's thinly sliced *hammour*, the endangered but oh-so-delicious local grouper fish. There's *ika natto*, cuttlefish with fermented soybeans, and fatty tuna that looks positively marbled. Along with the NHK channel on the TV and the clink of sake glasses hitting the tables, all the classics of a hardworking Japanese bar are present: *agedashi* tofu, smooth and creamy, capped with prodigious amounts of bonito flakes; vinegar-drenched seaweed; a nice, crisp dish of burdock root. Most of all, there's "tubular fried fish cake," which defies all interpretation but leaves us in awe of its many clashing textures and its singular wistful note of the sea.

Welcome to the Desert of the Real

Another friend of Nader's joins us for dinner, and herein we run into an interesting dilemma. Fresh from his long day working for a financial company, his friend is wearing the traditional white *kandora*. The bars that Nader wants to take us to, however, do not allow men in "national dress." This seems like the ultimate irony—U.A.E. citizens not allowed to enter a bar in their native land.

And so those of us in Western dress head for the African Garage Club, in the Ramee International Hotel in Nasser Square. Entering the democratic confines of the Garage after spending half the day begging for admittance to the world's tallest building is like falling

The Dubai Mall Aquarium. Above: Armani/ Ristorante's black-truffle spaghetti.

from the stratosphere into a small but welcome oasis. Everything here is sweaty and human and real. The theme is vaguely automotive. The clientele sit in hollowed-out cars, and the bar at the back is fitted inside the windows of an ancient bus, perhaps imported from Africa or the subcontinent. There's a portrait of Jimi Hendrix over the stage, supervising some serious guitar- and drum-driven South African jams. On the dance floor, the women are dancing so hard, they're practically doing push-ups.

We peel off from the Garage on a highway that sparkles with decorations for the Eid al-Adha holiday, the Feast of the Sacrifice. At night, the Burj Khalifa is as good a skyscraper as it gets, sparkly like tinsel, monumental like the Empire State Building. All alone up there above the malls and the sands, it looks like it could use a friend.

The Best Meal in Dubai

Nouf's mother is from Lebanon, a country with a cuisine of such sophistication that it often startles me that every other restaurant in the world does not serve meze. Al Nafoorah, the Lebanese restaurant in the Jumeirah Emirates Towers, is just an elevator ride away from me, but it is by far the best meal I will have in Dubai. During the colder (read: still insanely hot) months, it is possible to dine outdoors beneath the lit-up palms. The air is infused with scent. You can smell Al Nafoorah's tasty hookahs and charcoal grill from a skyscraper away.

My method here is to take a puff of the mint-grape *shisha,* take a sip of martini (in the Lebanese style this is simply Martini-brand vermouth, served, for some reason, in a margarita glass), eat something completely unexpected, and then listen to Nouf explaining what on earth I just ate. There are the sautéed chicken livers drizzled with pomegranate sauce, the smoothest, tastiest chicken livers I've ever had. "The richness of the liver is like a narcotic," Nouf says, "but the sharpness of the pomegranate keeps you awake." *Muhammara* means "reddened," she explains, as in the gorgeous dip of chili paste, bread crumbs, walnuts, and olive oil that I follow up with puffs of smoke, letting the mint from the *shisha* hit the back of my scalded palate. Then there are tiny birds—*assafir,* pan-fried ortolan—again in pomegranate sauce, a little finger snack from heaven, though those who object to swallowing an entire animal in one bite should give it a wide berth. "It's like you're eating fried chicken in reverse," Nouf says, because the crunch comes at the very end. The dishes pile up. A pickle platter bearing turnip, cauliflower, and Armenian bitter melon. Cold minced lamb with raw onion. Freshly sautéed dandelion root with onion and olive oil. All this bounty is scooped up with *saj,* a paper-thin unleavened bread that makes ordinary pita look stupid. By the end of the meal I am a confirmed mezeholic.

"Do You Have the Code?"

Oh, God, not again. Nouf and I are standing at the edge of Madinat Jumeirah, an enormous resort comprising 80 acres of Arabian-themed insanity. We are trying to get to Pierchic, the resort's seafood restaurant built at the end of a long pier. The restaurant has not sent me the code. But I do have a room key to the Jumeirah Emirates Towers, a sister hotel, which impresses a man in uniform enough so that we are allowed in; that is to say, we are deemed of the right class. After 30 minutes of walking across innumerable bridges, bumping into a strange Thai statue that I mistake for a waitress and try to reason with, and catching a lift from a buggy driven by a Hindi-speaking man, we arrive at Pierchic.

The restaurant is most perfect in the dark, with the sail of the Burj Al Arab twinkling in the near distance, its helipad perched over the water like an offering plate, tables of well-heeled French and English families floating through the night alongside us. From this vantage point, Dubai after sunset looks interplanetary. We hear the slap of the waves against the pier, and the slap of fish in the water, and order a pan-fried sea bass and an equally pan-fried halibut. The best part of the meal lives under the sea bass, a mash of veal bacon and Savoy cabbage that we pick at for an hour while the worried server hovers over us with the eternal Dubai question: "Is everything to your liking, Mr. Gary?"

Before we arrived at Pierchic, Nouf and I had been to a birthday party at 360° Bar at the Jumeirah Beach Hotel, another off-shore establishment in the shadow of the Burj Al Arab. There, we met Texan pilots, French skydiving instructors, and entire platoons of pink-faced, Dockers-wearing U.K. and Commonwealth expats. Between the inhalations of copious amounts of expensive alcohol, the talk, as always, was of Dubai's ruling family, the most fascinating topic in the Emirates.

"They own four 737's."

"They use a C-130 as a station wagon."

"They go falconing in Pakistan."

"They have a private island and they stop military air traffic when the crown prince needs a lift home."

"They see a restaurant they like in London or Paris and they just buy one for Dubai."

Back on the buggy to the mainland, a drunk Australian in a fedora and pink oxford shirt squeezes in next to me and drapes his arm around my shoulder. Pointing to the approaching skyline of Dubai, he shouts: "I *oin* this town! I bloody *oin* it!"

He's got the code.

Just For the Record

By now the reader may be wondering, Where is the best view of Dubai proper as seen from an establishment jutting out into the Gulf? The answer is: the 101 Bar at the One&Only The Palm resort, which hangs off the crescent of the enormous palm-shaped archipelago of artificial islands. This watering hole and restaurant is built on stilts, giving it a Seychelles kind of feel. It is entirely free of drunken expats, catering instead to a more sedate crowd, including the monied locals who actually "oin" this town. The view of the Dubai Marina lighting up the shoreline like an instant Manhattan is easily the most romantic in the city, unless you've brought your own yacht.

Czar Nicholas's Last Request

I begin the new day with a spicy, meaty breakfast at Ravi Restaurant, in the busy Satwa neighborhood, a stone's throw but a world away from Dubai's gleaming downtown. The Pakistani restaurant is a linoleum hole-in-the-wall, crammed with taxi drivers, low-level hotel staff, men in red worsted employee ties. There's a bag of chopped onions in the refrigerator, along with gallons of Mountain Dew. There are hungry men expertly folding naan like handkerchiefs before dipping them into pools of spice. I eat a *lula*-style mutton kebab just for the fun of it, but the real star of the show is the *nihari* stew, on the breakfast menu. It's the national dish of Pakistan: flaky, tender, just-off-the-bone meat studded with green peppercorns.

Slightly on fire, I stumble back to the Dubai Mall to visit the amazing new aquarium. Watching a tiger shark swim overhead is fun, but nothing beats the world's smartest otters, who give their trainers high fives and could probably do your taxes if you asked them nicely enough.

The sea animals have rekindled my hunger. It is time for one of my last meals in the emirate. It is time to head

GUIDE

STAY

Al Khaleej Palace Hotel
Al Makthoum Rd., Deira; alkhaleejpalace.net. $

Armani Hotel
Burj Khalifa, 1 Mohammed bin Rashid Blvd.; armanihotels.com. $$$$$

Burj Al Arab
Jumeirah Rd.; jumeirah.com. $$$$$

Jumeirah Emirates Towers
Sheikh Zayed Rd.; jumeirah.com. $$

Madinat Jumeirah
Jumeirah Rd.; jumeirah.com. $$$$

One&Only The Palm
West Crescent, Palm Island; oneandonlyresorts.com. $$$$

Towers Rotana Hotel Dubai
Sheikh Zayed Rd.; rotana.com. $

EAT AND DRINK

African Garage Club
Ramee International Hotel, Nasser Square, Deira; rameehotels.com.

Al Nafoorah
Jumeirah Emirates Towers; jumeirah.com. $$$

Armani/Ristorante
Armani Hotel; armanihotels.com. $$$$

At.mosphere Lounge
Burj Khalifa; atmosphereburjkhalifa.com. $$$

Kisaku Japanese Restaurant
Al Khaleej Palace Hotel; alkhaleejpalace.net. $$$$

101 Dining Lounge & Bar
One&Only The Palm; oneandonlyresorts.com. $$$

Pierchic
Madinat Jumeirah; jumeirah.com. $$$$

Ravi Restaurant
Satwa Rd.; 971-4/331-5353. $

Teatro
Towers Rotana Hotel Dubai; rotana.com. $$$$

360° Bar
Jumeirah Beach Hotel, Jumeirah Rd.; jumeirah.com.

On the terrace at 360° Bar, part of the Jumeirah Beach Hotel complex.

back to the Armani Hotel, in the Burj Khalifa next door. But now I know the drill. Now I have all the codes I'll ever need. Now I am Dubaian, smart as an otter.

I am joining Nader, the Rare Glory, for dinner at Armani/Ristorante. We enter the hushed, circular dining room with its tastefully beige décor. The nightly fountain show outside the artificial Burj Khalifa Lake is still going strong, and Nader points out the various dances being performed by the towering plumes of water: the Arabic Hair Dance, the Swinging Cane Dance. In deference to local excess, we decide to order nearly all of our dishes off the truffle menu. A part of me wants to write the rest of this article as a Tom Wolfe homage. He was eating! The most! Expensive! Black truffle! In! The world's! Tallest! Building! But I will restrain myself.

And then something happens that neither Nader nor I expect. The food proves to be as delicious as the view outside. The plump roasted scallops with celeriac and black truffle, the *stracciatella* cheese with artichoke, Parmesan, and black truffle—all are subject to slow chewing and contemplation. Nader

remarks upon the authentic lack of red sauce in the dish of wild-boar pappardelle. My eggy tagliolini with white truffles is al dente to the *massimo*. We order a toothsome red wine for under $100, which may be the greatest bargain I've yet encountered in Dubai. I scan the coast for a GENTLEMEN ARE EXPECTED TO SPEND AT LEAST $200 ON A BOTTLE OF CHIANTI sign, but there is none. All we have in front of us is calm: the oatmeal tablecloth, the golden menus.

For dessert, we are presented with *la sfera*, which is essentially an edible Fabergé egg, made with vanilla cream, violet crème brûlée, and cassis sorbet. If poor Czar Nicholas II had been granted a last request, this would have been a good choice.

"I didn't know dessert could be so good with truffle," the tall Russian hostess exclaims to me as we leave.

"Everything taste good with zeh truffle," I want to tell her, in my new Dubaian accent, which is neither Russian nor American, but filled with rich, truffle-like sibilants. Give me a few more weeks. I'll *oin* this town. +

Sharing a bowl
of beef *pho* at
Quan An Ngon, in
Hanoi, Vietnam.

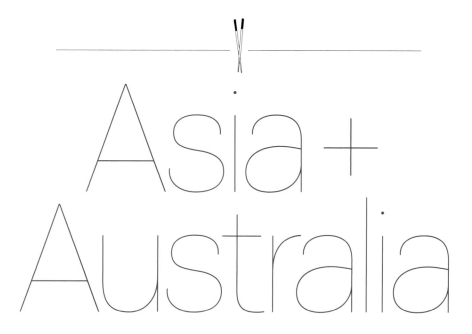

Asia + Australia

The Ultimate Vietnamese Food Tour

BY PETER JON LINDBERG / PHOTOGRAPHED BY BROWN W. CANNON III

Riding past a roadside flower market in the countryside near Hanoi.

Bánh cuon (pork-and-shrimp dumplings) from a street-food vendor at Hanoi's Quan An Ngon.

"*AN COM CHUA?*" If you're going to understand Vietnam and the Vietnamese, this three-word phrase is key. A friendly greeting exchanged throughout the day, it poses a seemingly mundane question: "Have you eaten yet?" (The polite answer, even if you have, is "Why, no—let's eat!") Food is at the very heart of Vietnamese culture. Almost every aspect of social, devotional, and family life revolves around the procurement, preparation, and shared pleasure of nourishment. Even commercial life: more than half of Vietnam's population makes a living in agriculture or the food trade. Markets are on every corner; cooks on every curb. A sneeze elicits the blessing *com muoi,* or "rice with salt."

On a recent train ride from Hue to Hoi An, food was everywhere in sight. At each station stop, vendors rushed up to the windows proffering homemade treats: shrimp cakes, jerky, sticky rice. One vendor came aboard and walked the aisles, selling sun-dried squid. (An American traveler bought one, thinking it was a decorative fan.) In the bar car the train conductor and his staff spent the whole ride not collecting tickets but preparing lunch: cooking noodles, shelling prawns, trimming basil into woven baskets.

Follow any lane in any Vietnamese city at any time of day and you'll find some contented soul crouched over a bowl of broth or rice. Then again, if you lived in Vietnam, you'd eat all the damn time, too. The food is beautiful to behold, if only for the colors alone: turmeric-yellow crêpes, sunset-orange crabs, scarlet-red chiles, deep-purple shrimp paste, and endless jungles of vivid green. Vietnamese cooking is fresher, healthier, lighter, and brighter than, for instance, Chinese or Indian or French, three of its closest relations. Though it is often described as "honest" and "direct"—cooks resist fussy ornamentation (except in Hue; more on that later)—this is a cuisine rich with nuance, carrying a complexity that is all the more surprising for its being served in, say, a plastic bowl with a Tweety Bird logo, on a flimsy table on the pavement. Flavors and textures are deftly arranged so each note rings clear, from the piercing highs of chili paste and *nuoc mam* (fish sauce) to the bottomless depths of a stock that's been burbling since dawn. These are tastes that sate, soothe, and just as often shock you awake—particularly the pungent greens and herbs that figure in almost every dish. After the wonder that is Vietnamese produce, the stuff back home seems like a recording of a recording of a cassette that was left out in the sun.

HANOI

I've spent roughly 100 days in Hanoi over the past 12 years, and I don't recall ever once seeing blue sky. Not that I'd have it any other way. Like London or Seattle, this is a city that becomes itself under cloud cover. During those moist, moody afternoons, when mist hangs over the streets like smoke from a cooking fire, Vietnam's gorgeous old capital feels more intimate than it already is.

Even in the heat of summer, Hanoians favor cockle-warming dishes suited to far chillier climes. The most renowned of these is Vietnam's de facto national dish: *pho bo,* eaten at any time of day but especially for breakfast. Taking root in an earthy, long-simmered beef broth—shot through with clove, ginger, and star anise—the soup is filled out with rice noodles and one or more varieties of raw or cooked beef, tendon, or tripe.

The walkway to the Ngoc Son Temple, in Hanoi's Hoan Kiem Lake. Right: Ms. Thai, owner of Café Nang, in Hanoi.

A Hanoi street scene. Left: A bowl of beef *pho* at Hanoi's Pho Gia Truyen.

Southerners sprinkle fresh herbs and bean sprouts on top, but a Northern *pho* is generally unadorned, with only a few scallions and a bit of cilantro cooked into the broth and perhaps a squirt of rice vinegar.

Pho Gia Truyen, on Bat Dan Street in Hanoi's Old Quarter, doesn't look like much from the outside—or from the inside, for that matter. The room has a clock, two fans, three bare lightbulbs, and a handful of communal tables. The only decoration is the food itself: hulking slabs of brisket suspended from hooks, a hillside of scallions on the counter, and a giant cauldron puffing out fragrant clouds of steam like some benevolent dragon. A cashier takes your money (about a dollar a serving), her colleague fills a bowl with noodles and chopped scallions, and a teenager with a faux-hawk ladles strips of ruby-red beef into the broth to cook for two seconds, then spoons it all into the waiting bowl. Half of Hanoi queues up for a seat, while others slurp

Cultivating rice in Bac Ninh, a village outside Hanoi. Below: At the Citadel in Hue.

Follow any lane in any Vietnamese city at any time of day and you'll find some contented soul crouched over a bowl of broth or rice.

their soup perched on motorbikes outside. All wear serious expressions, and eat in a silence that feels not joyless but reverential. The stock is so wholesome and protein-rich you feel yourself being cured of whatever might ail you, perhaps of anything that ever could.

A proper restaurant culture, the sort with waitstaff and normal-size chairs, is still in its infancy here, but Vietnam has a long tradition of eating out—quite literally so. Western notions of indoors and out are reversed: at a typical Old Quarter house in Hanoi, the motorbikes are in the living room and the stove is on the sidewalk.

When people here crave a particular dish, they usually visit a particular street vendor, often on a particular lane (which may even be named after said dish). The best way to tackle Hanoi is to treat the city as one vast progressive buffet, moving from the spring-roll guy to the fermented-pork lady and onward into the

night. (For an exhaustive guide to Hanoi's top street stalls, check out stickyrice.typepad.com.)

Or you could make it easy and hit Quan An Ngon (locals call it simply "Ngon," meaning delicious). The owner recruited an all-star roster of street-food vendors to cook their signature dishes in the courtyard of an old villa, added menus and table service, and watched the crowds pour in—not just foreigners but also well-heeled Vietnamese, who can't get enough of the place. (There's also a branch in Saigon, a.k.a Ho Chi Minh City.) The quality is excellent, the atmosphere convivial, and seats hard to come by after dark. Arrive for breakfast and the food is even fresher (and the cooks outnumber the patrons). Most of these dishes are traditionally served all day, so the morning menu is much the same. My ultimate breakfast: an order of *bun cha* (grilled pork in a sweet sauce with a side of rice vermicelli) and a bowl of *bánh da ca*, a fabulously tangy fish soup from Haiphong laden with chunks of tilapia, chewy, fettucine-like *bánh da* noodles, dill, scallions, and the magical *rau can* (a woody stalk with a strong, cedary bite).

Speaking of fish, Hanoi *cha ca* is one of the great Vietnamese dishes, a note-perfect blend of raw and cooked ingredients, assertive and delicate flavors, with a DIY element as a bonus. It's often associated with a century-old Hanoi institution called Cha Ca La Vong, which is very good, indeed, though I prefer the more peaceful surroundings and local clientele of its rival, Cha Ca Thang Long, a few blocks away. The firm white flesh of the snakehead fish is first marinated in galangal, shallot, shrimp paste, and turmeric, and briefly seared on a grill. It's then brought to your table in a large pan with bowls of shaved scallions, crumbled peanuts, chiles, and a hedgerow of bright-green dill. A tabletop brazier is ignited. This is where you come in: tossing everything into the sizzling pan, sautéing the fish to a golden brown, then laying it onto a bed of cool vermicelli, with a few more dill sprigs for good measure. Add a dollop of supremely funky shrimp paste if you dare (and you should).

For all their obsessive eating and snacking, Hanoians tend not to linger at the table. Most finish dinner in seven minutes flat. Where they do while away the hours is at the local café. Hanoians drink a *lot* of coffee:

thick, rich, tar-black stuff, sometimes cut with condensed milk but often taken straight. The bohemian soul of Hanoi's café scene is Nang, a 1956 landmark on Hang Bac Street whose 74-year-old owner, Ms. Thai, still brews nearly every cup herself. (Her father-in-law, who lived in Paris for a spell, taught her how to French-roast the beans.) Ms. Thai's blend, sourced from Dong Giao, in the northern Nghe An province, is strong enough to power a 125 cc motorbike. The café is only eight feet wide, with tiny wooden tables and tinier wooden stools, occupied all afternoon by young Vietnamese men sporting the currently in vogue greaser look: slicked-back hair, black leather jackets, skinny jeans, white pocket T's with single cigarettes poking out. The place looks exactly as it must have in 1956—a perfect microcosm of a city that's always had a tenuous relation to the present tense.

HUE

Hue is a slow-burn town. While Vietnam's former imperial capital is certainly beautiful (the flame trees lining the boulevards could make a grown man swoon), it's also sleepy and standoffish, more village than city. There's an upside to this: a short bike ride out from the center will bring you into unkempt wilderness, where only cicadas break the silence. But downtown isn't much livelier. And though Hue figures into plenty of travelers' itineraries—for its magnificent Citadel, pagodas, and imperial tombs—many find it tough to crack.

In all my visits I never really "got" Hue, until I met Vo Thi Huong Lan, a friend of a friend who offered to show me its elusive charms. Lan is something of a professional enthusiast (her three favorite words: "I love it!") and is positively mad for her hometown. "They say Hue is a place you leave, so you can miss it when you're gone," she told me, "but I never want to live anywhere else." Most of all, she's crazy about the food. Hue is renowned for its elaborate cuisine, developed by the skilled cooks of the royal court. Legend has it that the Nguyen kings, who ruled a united Vietnam from Hue in the 19th century, refused to eat the same meal twice in a year, so their cooks came up with hundreds of distinct, visually arresting dishes (most using the same few dozen ingredients). This tradition endures in the local craze for dainty, flower-like dumplings and cakes such as *bánh beo,* which aesthetically owe much to China and Japan. *Bánh beo* is an acquired taste ("I love it!" Lan says), a bit too gluey for my own; it may be the only Vietnamese food I don't enjoy.

But I was knocked out by Hue's other specialties, from *com hen* (a spicy clam-and-rice concoction) to *bánh khoai* (a fajita-size rice-flour crêpe similar to the Southern favorite *bánh xeo*). Lan, it turns out, eats like a five-foot-tall Anthony Bourdain, reveling in the bottom of the food chain: pig intestines, chicken heads ("I love the brains!"), and shrimp eyes ("My mother says if you eat them, your own eyes will brighten"). For breakfast at Quan Cam, we tucked into a stellar *bun bo Hue,* the city's signature dish: a fiery broth of long-simmered beef bones, suffused with lemongrass and stained red from chiles, ladled over a bowlful of umami: paper-thin strips of beef, crab-and-pork meatballs, pig's trotters, and *huyet*—quivering cubes of

---

The stock at Pho Gia Truyen is so wholesome you feel yourself being cured of whatever ails you, perhaps of anything that ever could.

congealed pig's blood. (These are way, way better than they sound.) The *bun bo* is served only until 9:30 a.m., so early mornings are the busiest time. Some customers grabbed takeaway portions in skimpy plastic bags tied with a string. Lan, meanwhile, gobbled up *huyet* like so many Snickers bars ("I love it!"), then cast a still-hungry eye on my bowl: "Are you going to finish that?"

In the leafy enclave of Kim Long, we lunched at the open-air canteen Huyen Anh, which serves two dishes only: *bánh uot thit nuong* and *bun thit nuong.* The former, dim sum–like ravioli stuffed with grilled pork, are terrific. But it's Huyen Anh's *bun thit nuong* that sums up everything that's simple and delightful about Vietnamese cooking. *Bun* means noodles—in this case a bowl of vermicelli—that arrive still warm and soft, with a moistening drizzle of *nuoc cham* (fish sauce and lime juice infused with clove, chili, and garlic). Shaved banana blossoms, shredded lettuce, bean sprouts,

peanuts, cucumber, and green papaya provide a textural counterpoint, while sprigs of cilantro and aggressive peppermint fill in the high end. The crowning touch: glistening slices of char-grilled pork. At home in New York I used to order *bun thit nuong* twice a week at our local Viet kitchen; alas, Huyen Anh's has ruined me for anyone else's.

HOI AN

It's true that the quaint, narrow streets of this fishing village turned backpacker mecca turned resort haven are often choked with tour buses. But Hoi An still evokes Vietnam's long-ago like few places can, especially at night, when the lanes are finally quiet and silk lanterns glimmer like rainbows off the river. Like Hue, Hoi An has a fine culinary tradition, including some dishes that are only made (or made well) here. One is the soup known as *cao lau,* whose thick noodles are cooked in water from one of five local wells. Any other water, people tell you, just won't work.

Because Hoi An is still a town of fishermen—at least those who haven't taken jobs at luxury hotels—it's a fantastic place for fresh seafood. On nearby Cua Dai Beach, barbecue restaurants have set up tables in the sand; the best of the lot is the amiable, family-run Hon, whose *muc nuong* (grilled squid) and *ngheu hap* (clams with ginger, lemongrass, and fresh mint) are both ridiculously good.

The doyenne of Hoi An's food scene is Trinh Diem Vy, whom everyone calls Ms. Vy. The 43-year-old chef owns four restaurants here, the flagship of which is Morning Glory, a bustling two-story house in the heart of the Old Town. Morning Glory is a tourist haunt, and proudly so. It's also the best place in town to sample Hoi An cuisine. While you can get a very good *cao lau* from stalls at the Hoi An market, Morning Glory's rendition is endlessly richer: a tangy broth spiked with anise and soy sauce, sprinkled with chives, mint, and cilantro, and topped with a crumbled rice cracker. In the center are juicy strips of *thit xiu* (soy-simmered pork, pronounced sa-syoo, as in the Chinese *char siu*). Ms. Vy's *cao lau* noodles are so toothsome and chewy you'd swear you were eating soba, not rice noodles.

But what Hoi An is mainly known for is *bánh mì.* Vietnam's iconic sandwich is rarely served in

Fishing along Hue's Perfume River. Right: *Bun thit nuong* (grilled pork with vermicelli) from Huyen Anh.

restaurants, but sold from bakery counters and street carts. The term (pronounced bun mee) refers to the baguette itself; the sandwich is formally a *bánh mì thit pâté* (*thit* = meat, *pâté* = pâté) or sometimes a *bánh mì thit nuong* (*thit nuong* = grilled meat). In the classic version, the pâté—a rich, velvety, offal-y spread— is paired with smoky barbecued pork and/or some mortadella-like cold cuts. Atop that goes a slathering of mayonnaise, strips of pickled carrot and daikon, cucumber, chiles, a few sprigs of cilantro, and behold: the best sandwich ever.

That's what I used to think, anyway. But no prior encounter could have prepared me for the marvel of Phuong Bánh Mi, a sandwich stand on Hoang Dieu Street run by a young woman of the same name. I'd heard about Phuong from friends in Hanoi and Saigon. The concierge at the Nam Hai resort practically growled with hunger when I mentioned the place. Phuong's *bánh mì* is unique in that (a) she adds sliced tomato and hand-ground chili sauce, along with the standard trimmings; and (b) unlike in the South, where the baguettes are inflated to balloon-like proportions, Phuong's are modestly sized, the bread-to-filling ratio spot-on. Come in the early morning or late afternoon (after the second baking) and the bread is still warm. Phuong wraps her creations in newspaper if you want them to go, but I devoured mine right there on the curb in about 47 seconds. It was unbefreakinglievable.

HO CHI MINH CITY (SAIGON)

Ahh, the South. Everything is hotter: the air, the chiles, the woks, the fashion. Beer is served with a big chunk of ice; it melts before you're finished. Compared with the food up North, the dishes are generally lighter—the heat, again—and sweeter. (Southerners have a predilection for coconut milk, sugarcane, and saccharine desserts.) And while Northerners might call Southern cuisine unsophisticated, its origins are varied and complex. Unlike Hanoi, a more insular city whose identity is decidedly Vietnamese, Saigon has always had one foot in the outside world—just as the world has always had at least one foot in Saigon. Foreign influences are readily absorbed here, from the Indian and Malay flavors that inspired Southern-style

Shopping for flowers and fresh produce in Hanoi.

ca ry (curry) to the Singaporean noodle shops now favored by Saigon teenagers.

This is an upwardly mobile city, consumed with money and ways to show it off, and its dining scene is accordingly flashier, more cosmopolitan. Alas, things change quickly in these boom times; every year or two I return to Saigon to find that more old favorites have disappeared. Thankfully, some touchstones remain—including my beloved crab joint, Quan Thuy 94. With an industrial fan roaring in the corner and a Jason Statham movie cranking on the TV, it's short on visible charm. But the staff is adorable, and the kitchen knows the hell out of crab. The soft-shells, coated in lip-puckering tamarind sauce, burst in the mouth to unleash a creamy, tangy sweetness. *Cha gio cua* (crab spring rolls) are fried to an unerringly calibrated crunch. The unmissable order is *mien xao cua be*: glass noodles sautéed with crabmeat, mushrooms, chiles, and vermilion-colored crab roe. (A word about the name: Quan Thuy 94 used to be at 94 Dinh Tien Hoang. When it moved down the street to No. 84, it kept "94" in its name. Confusing things further, a whole new crab joint has taken the old No. 94 storefront—but it's No. 84 you want. Got that? Onward.)

While the city evolves relentlessly around them, Saigon's traditional street-food stalls provide a rare sense of continuity. High-rise hotels and IMAX theaters might shoot up next door, but the iconic sidewalk cook keeps plying her trade, unfazed. Case in point: Nguyen Thi Thanh, known as The Lunch Lady. For 13 years, Monday through Saturday, she has set up shop on a patch of pavement on Hoang Sa Street near the zoo—working from 11 a.m. until she runs out of food, which happens quickly. Office workers, schoolkids, and housewives queue up for whatever Lunch Lady is serving that day: usually noodles of some sort, invariably delicious. Wednesdays she often cooks up a knockout *hu tieu*, a Southern noodle soup laden with roasted sliced pork, prawns, peanuts, and soft-cooked quail eggs; the smoky broth is flavored with shallots and dried squid. It's a family affair: from an adjacent stand, Lunch Lady's cousin sells *goi cuon*, fresh summer rolls filled with sweet shrimp. Nearby, another relative blends ripe, fragrant tropical fruit into icy *sinh to* (smoothies).

Fruit, in fact, might be the single best thing about eating here. Saigon's proximity to the Mekong Delta—which supplies fully half of Vietnam's produce—means the city overflows with papaya, mango, coconut, jackfruit, soursop, and other exotic treats. Wildly colorful fruit stands are on every other corner, their artfulness rivaling the displays at Takashimaya. Even at Ben Thanh Market, where rapacious vendors sell watered-down food, the *sinh to* stands are uniformly fantastic. I've had few more refreshing drinks than the smoothie I tried at Ben Thanh one sultry 97-degree afternoon, made with sapodilla fruit and avocado.

Hanoi may lay claim to its invention, but plenty of *pho* lovers (including myself) favor the Southern incarnation, which uses fresh herbs and raw greens for a broader range of textures. For years I've scoured the back alleys of Saigon, trying to find a better version than that served at Pho Hoa on Pasteur Street, but to no avail: this tour group–friendly institution really does serve the tastiest *pho* in town. To get the full experience you need to come early for breakfast, when the clientele is all Vietnamese. *Pho tai nam* is your order, with rare beef and well-done flank (recalling a thick-sliced pastrami). In genuine Southern style, dress it with bean sprouts, hoisin sauce, chili sauce, a squirt of lime, and leaves from the heaping platter of basil, sawtooth

coriander, and rice-paddy herb, whose tiny leaves pack a cumin-like punch. Now it's 7:15, and you're ready for your first cup of coffee.

Herbs and greens are also integral to a Saigon *bánh xeo* (pronounced bun *say*-o, meaning "sizzling cake"). This rice-flour crêpe is reminiscent of an Indian *dosa*, but wider, and yellow with turmeric—bright as the sun and nearly as big. Guidebooks will send you to 46A Dinh Cong Trang, an alley-side joint in District 3. But a better version can be found at Bánh Xeo An La Ghien (loosely translated as "eat and be addicted"). Into an outsize wok the chef tosses a fistful of bean sprouts, pork, shrimp, and/or mushrooms, then pours in a slick of marigold-yellow batter, rich with coconut milk. The resulting crêpe is the size of a Monopoly board—so large it overwhelms the table, let alone the plate. Its crisp, lacy edges break off with a satisfying crackle, complementing the moist and savory fillings. The key elements, however, are the pile of fresh herbs to tuck inside the crêpe and the giant mustard leaves to wrap the thing in; their aroma and bite are as powerful as a jarful of Dijon.

t's not hard to find great street food in Saigon: just walk 10 steps in any direction and pull up a stool. Nor is it hard to find, say, some sumptuously decorated dining room in some gorgeous 19th-century villa where the waft

GUIDE

EAT
HANOI
Café Nang
6 Hang Bac St.;
84-4/3824-0459.

Cha Ca La Vong
14 Pho Cha Ca;
84-4/3825-3929. $

Cha Ca Thang Long
31 Duong Thanh;
84-4/3824-5115;
chacathanglong.com. $

Chau Long Market
Corner of Chau Long and
Nguyen Sts.

Pho Gia Truyen
(a.k.a. Pho 49 Bat Dan)
49 Bat Dan St.; no phone. $

Quan An Ngon
18 Phan Boi Chau St.;
84-4/3942-8162;
ngonhanoi.com.vn. $

HUE
Huyen Anh
52/1 Kim Long St.;
84-54/352-5655. $

Quan Cam
38 Tran Cao Van St.;
84-54/383-1671. $

HOI AN
Bánh Mì Phuong
Hoang Dieu St. (on the way
to Cam Nam Bridge,
right-hand side); no phone. $

Hon
Stall No. 9, Cua Dai Beach
(off Lac Long Quan St.);
84-510/392-7272. $

Morning Glory Restaurant
106 Nguyen Thai Hoc St.;
84-510/224-1555;
restaurant-hoian.com. $$

HO CHI MINH CITY
(SAIGON)
Bánh Xeo An La Ghien
74 Suong Nguyet Anh St.;
84-8/3833-0534;
bánhxeoanlaghien.com.vn. $

Ben Thanh Market
Intersection of Le Loi and
Tran Hung Dao Sts.

Cuc Gach Quan
10 Dang Tat, Tan Dinh Ward;
84-8/3848-0144;
cucgachquan.com.vn. $

Nguyen Thi Thanh
(The Lunch Lady)
Street stall near 23 Hoang Sa
St.; no phone. $

Pho Hoa
260C Pasteur St.;
84-8/3829-7943. $

Quan An Ngon
160 Pasteur St.;
84-8/3827-7131. $

Quan Thuy 94
84 Dinh Tien Hoang St.;
84-8/3910-1062. $

Cuon diep (shrimp rolls) at Cuc Gach Quan, in Ho Chi Minh City. Left: The restaurant's owners, Tran Binh and his wife, Thai Tu-Tho.

of jasmine incense and a warble of jazz help distract from the blandness of the food. The hard part is finding atmosphere and authenticity in the same package. According to what I call the Law of Inverse Relation, the tastiest food is served in the least inviting venues, and vice versa. (A good rule: incandescent lights = order drinks only; fluorescent lights = eat here now.)

That all held true until, by some blissful accident on a recent trip, three friends and I stumbled upon the exception: Cuc Gach Quan ("the brick house"), owned by architect Tran Binh and his French-Vietnamese wife, Thai Tu-Tho. Binh acquired a derelict colonial mansion and reimagined it as an indoor-outdoor fantasia, blending historic details (antique armoires; a wall map of 1960's Saigon) with contemporary touches (gorgeous lighting; a floating staircase) to create a strikingly romantic space—a gauzy, soft-focus realm that plays with one's sense of time. Pre-1975 Vietnamese folk plays on a vintage reel-to-reel tape machine. A flowering cherry tree in the courtyard provides the fragrance.

But again: graceful interiors are a dime a dozen in Saigon. It's the cooking that makes Cuc Gach Quan remarkable. From an open kitchen, the chefs, Co Diep and Chi Bay, sent out a phenomenal *thit kho to*, or clay-pot-stewed pork belly; intensely flavored but not at all heavy, it tingled the tongue then melted in the mouth. Eggplant cooked in scallion oil was deliciously smoky and tender. Diep's cloudlike house-made tofu was lightly fried with lemongrass, shallots, and chiles, creating a sauce worth bottling and smuggling home. This was not showy, dazzle-me cuisine, but more like the *com binh danh* (worker's food) that Vietnamese enjoy every day. "My grandmother used to cook like this," said my friend Anh with a sigh. "Just not as well."

It was clear that every detail had been considered, from the handsome tin canister that held the chopsticks to the fresh juice service, with a stalk of morning glory for a straw. Yet nothing felt labored or pretentious. There was an ease and simplicity to the service and the food that belied the elegance of the setting. Most of all there was joy. And as Duy Khanh crooned a sweet nostalgic ballad on the reel-to-reel, we all felt entirely at home. ✚

Shanghai

China's most cosmopolitan city is in the throes of a restaurant revolution. While regional cuisine still reigns in dining rooms across town, a group of expat chefs are rewriting the rules on Italian, French, and American food. Here, seven places that epitomize the best of East and West.

Hai by Goga

At his first restaurant, Goga, San Francisco native Brad Turley gained a cult following for his spot-on Pacific Rim cuisine and California-centric wine list. His second act sticks to the same formula: boldly flavored dishes such as tuna-edamame potato salad and scallops with Thai lobster curry. Then there's the creative cocktail menu. Choose from juniper-berry-and-Kaffir-lime-leaf-infused gin and tonics, martinis studded with pumpkin-packed olives, and bourbon punctuated by caramelized pineapples and vanilla bean. *1 Yueyang Rd., seventh floor; 86-21/3461-7893.* **$$$**

Jishi

When it comes to authentic Shanghainese food, you can't do better than Jishi, a tiny, unpretentious restaurant in the Former French Concession. (Be prepared: waiters speak nary a word of English.) The old-school dishes continue to draw perennial lines of locals looking to feast on such staples as *tangcu paigu* (sweet-and-sour spareribs) and *congbao yutou* (braised fish head with scallions). If it's hairy-crab season (October–December), don't miss the *xiefen fenpi,* wok-fried crab with vermicelli sheets. *41 Tianping Lu; 86-21/6282-9260.* **$$**

Lost Heaven

In a 1920's villa on a quiet street in the Former French Concession, moody lighting, Buddhist sculptures, and carved-teak chairs set the backdrop for the city's finest Yunnanese cuisine—a culinary education in the traditional recipes of the native Dai and Miao tribes. On the menu: mouthwatering lemongrass-laced meats, crisp vegetable pancakes, and spicy curries loaded with a variety of indigenous mushrooms. After your meal, grab a nightcap in the first-floor lounge, decorated with stone folk masks from the Mekong Delta. *38 Gaoyou Rd.; 86-21/6433-5126; lostheaven.com.cn.* **$$**

Madison

An alum of New York's Gramercy Tavern, young chef Austin Hu is spearheading the city's locavore movement with ingredients sourced almost entirely from nearby purveyors, from the fava beans to the Sinkiang Black beer. At this loftlike space in the Xuhui district, standout dishes include chilled prawns with cilantro yogurt and preserved onion and a rich duck-breast salad with roasted apples and chorizo-flecked vinaigrette. Just as good is the weekend brunch next door, where a lively crowd floods sister bistro Madi's for comfort food such as chicken and waffles and pig's-trotter-croquette eggs Benedict. *3 Fenyang Rd., Bldg. 2; 86-21/6437-0136; madisoninshanghai.com.* **$$$**

Mercato

Jean-Georges Vongerichten teamed up with Shanghai-based design duo Neri & Hu at the rustic-chic Mercato, a Bund-side Italian restaurant done in reclaimed wood and leather. Fresh pastas (try the casareccie with mushroom Bolognese) and wood-fired pizzas top the menu, but there are also plenty of fish options—try the red snapper with braised fennel, carrots, and Cerignola olives. If a snack is all you're after, order the house-made ricotta on grilled bread, garnished with strawberry compote and drizzled with olive oil. *No. 3, Zhong Shan Dong Yi Rd., sixth floor; 86-21/6321-9922; threeonthebund.com.* **$$$**

Mr. & Mrs. Bund—Modern Eatery by Paul Pairet

On the sixth floor of a Neoclassical–style bank building, chef Paul Pairet's innovative French plates are full of whimsical touches: the tuna mousse is served in a peeled-back tin can; citrusy Boston lobster arrives at the table inside a glass Mason jar. Prefer something more traditional? Opt for the duck foie gras crumble and teriyaki-glazed long short ribs. *18 The Bund, sixth floor; 86-21/6323-9898; mmbund.com.* **$$$$**

Ultraviolet by Paul Pairet

Chef Pairet's latest endeavor takes his flair for culinary eccentricity to another level. With the help of projectors, scent diffusers, and a sophisticated sound system, he combines audio, olfactory, and visual effects for a multisensory experience that amplifies his four-hour, 22-course degustation meal. Expect offbeat dishes with wacky names such as "foie gras can't quit," a cigarette-shaped candy shell stuffed with foie gras mousse and cabbage ash; and "truffle burnt soup bread," one side dipped in soy butter, the other grilled and topped with truffles, presented in a glass dome of cigar smoke. Call it dinner theater for the 21st century. *86-21/6142-5198; uvbypp.cc.* **$$$$**

Garnishing Mercato's cheesecake. Left: Setting the table before guests arrive at Ultraviolet by Paul Pairet.

Madison's pork loin with brussels sprouts and hickory mustard. Right: The pizza counter at Mercato.

Traditional *tonkotsu*-style ramen at Mengekijo Genei, in the southern Japanese city of Fukuoka.

For the Love of Ramen

BY ADAM SACHS
PHOTOGRAPHED BY TETSUYA MIURA

I am on a plane, crossing an ocean to eat a soup made of pork bones. Mid-flight, I dream of my first encounter. Of the first slurp, revelatory as a first kiss. Of steam rising off the fat-slicked surface, the hot mishmash of chewy noodles and the just-set egg spilling its sunsetty yolk into the porky depths that are touched with the tang of sea and soy and miso and whatever proprietary, body- and mind-altering secrets have been stirred into the mix by the cooks at that pocket-size, second-floor shop in Omotesando that has a line up the stairs and down the block.

Locals in Fukuoka's Daimyo area. Left: Ramen at Shifuku (429), in Fukuoka.

A street scene in Fukuoka's Nakasu neighborhood. Right: A *sundo* (soup pot) on display at Shifuku (429).

You don't forget your first time with *tonkotsu* ramen. Mine happened a decade ago. Cold, gray Tokyo lunchtime in December. The first, skeptical spoonful. (What's all the fuss about?) Then the full rush of pure rendered meaty umami-ness. (Where has this been all my life?)

It is not a normal smell, the smell of *tonkotsu* ramen. The odor (no one would call it a fragrance) does not tip gently up the nasal passage. Rather, it sticks like a blow dart in the bridge of your nose. A sour, worrying foulness that speaks of some ancient, ancestral revulsion: this is how you first become aware of the proximity of true Hakata-style *tonkotsu* ramen. And it's precisely this strange funk that—once you've overcome the initial, misleading impression and fallen hard for the stuff—you find yourself dreaming about.

Since that first encounter, I've slouched over countless bowls of ramen, traditional and otherwise, in Tokyo—and sometimes in New York when the weather turns cool and I miss it. I've taken the train to Yokohama to visit the Ramen Museum. But I've never made it south to Fukuoka, a seaside city on the island of Kyushu, at the southwestern end of the country, to find the spiritual home of *tonkotsu*, the style of ramen that first opened my mind and staked its claim there of permanent longing. Memory propels me back. And also the plane. A plane is a must for crossing an ocean in time for dinner.

ADACHI WARD
12:45 a.m. Somewhere in the northern outskirts of Tokyo

I land in Tokyo late—and hungry. Happily, ramen shops keep insomniac hours, so I use my one-night layover to begin my ramen mission before flying to Kyushu in the morning. Tokyo's is a culture of everythingness: every regional variety of ramen delivered to the big stage of the capital city, then endlessly remixed and reinvented. You could fill every issue of this magazine for a year trying to describe the shape-shifting universe of Japanese ramen and you wouldn't get close to a complete picture. There are, in fact, many magazines devoted solely to ramen—and ramen TV shows, comic books, competitions.

Among the legion of ramen bloggers is my guide tonight, a 33-year-old California transplant named Brian MacDuckston. Gangly, personable, head shaved, smile full of braces, MacDuckston supports himself doing educational dance- and sing-alongs for kids; at night he documents his noodle addiction on his site, *Ramen Adventures*.

I ask MacDuckston to paint me a picture of the state of ramen in Tokyo these days. "There's a place called Papapapapine," he says. "Its speciality is pineapple ramen. Pineapple in the soup, pineapple in the toppings. What's goofy is, it works." Picture painted.

Rather than wade into the torrent of the new, I want to get right into the classical Kyushu swing of things, so MacDuckston steers us, by multiple subway connections, to the moonlit streets of a semi-industrial suburb. This is big-sky country by Tokyo standards.

We're looking for Tanaka Shoten, an out-of-the-way shop celebrated for its traditional Hakata-style ramen. We smell it before we see it.

Inside, we take our place at the bar and order a round of foam-topped draft beers. When the ramen is set before us, we lean our faces into the piggy *shvitz* of rising steam before getting to work slurping, splattering, and spooning up the milky, mouth-coatingly rich soup. Down the line, every head in the place is bowed in identical communion.

Noodle neophytes take note: ramen as it is served in the many thousands of steamy little shops and multiplying chains across Japan has nearly nothing in common with the denatured supermarket variant—brittle noodle-bricks and MSG-laced flavor dust. This kind of ramen exists in Japan, of course, in a vast universe of categories that would make even our novelty-addicted American minds explode. But the undergraduate-sustaining, just-add-water stuff has as much to do with real ramen as freeze-dried astronaut food has to do with flying to the moon.

Real ramen knocks you back a little and then sets you right on your feet. What we register as the "soup" component is really two things: the stock, which is cooked for many hours, and the *tare*, a reduced soy- or miso-based flavor-intensifying sauce that is introduced in small quantities just before the boiled noodles are dropped into the bowl. The stock is the soul of ramen; the *tare* its animating spirit. The stock is the steady thump of the rhythm section; *tare*, the soaring improvisational riffs of the horns. *Tonkotsu* refers to pork bones—and it is those long-boiled, marrow-rich, collagen-imparting pig parts that give the Hakata style (named for a neighborhood in Fukuoka) its distinctive stank and opaque creaminess and have spread its fame and influence to every ramen-crazed corner of Japan.

Behind the bar, a thick-armed dude with a towel tied round his head agitates a roiling cauldron with a wooden spoon as big as an oar. His damp T-shirt says POWER OF BONES. "He's beating the flavor out of those bones," MacDuckston says, dreamily.

MENGEKIJO GENEI
12 p.m. Tenjin Area, Fukuoka City

Japan's seventh-largest city has much to recommend it to the curious traveler and little evidence that anybody's been heeding the call. There are beaches, curving canals, sparkling shopping centers, and sweet, squat blocks of hip boutiques and coffee shops. *Monocle* magazine ranked it 12th in its Global Quality of Life Survey. Rem Koolhaas did a striking housing project here; Michael Graves, a lovely Hyatt.

Despite these charms, the city is not high on the foreign visitor's circuit. Even Japanese in the north seem to admire the idea of this relaxed southern city more than they actually come here.

My friend Shinji Nohara agreed to travel down from Tokyo, mainly because he knew we'd eat well.

Tonkotsu is Fukuoka's most famous culinary export and fans of the form will not be disappointed by the towering sight of the 12-story Ichiran building. Ichiran pioneered a style of ramen consumption that might be called solitary confinement with benefits: diners sit alone, separated in their sweaty-slurping-soup-inhaling isolation from one another by red-curtained dividers. Only in Japan could such a setup spawn a successful countrywide chain.

Ippudo is another estimable Fukuoka-founded brand, with outposts in Tokyo, Sydney, and New York City. The Manhattan shop is authentic down to the long lines out the door.

The originals are excellent, necessary stops on any *tonkotsu* pilgrimage. But I want to eat things I can't find elsewhere.

Mengekijo Genei, which occupies an angular, corrugated-steel structure that looks as if it might house a small architectural firm, fits this definition well. The seats are arranged like a tiny theater in the round, or a college science lab, each row higher than the one in front so that every diner has a clear view of center stage: the man boiling the noodles and ladling out the soup.

Hideki Irie, the charismatic chef-owner, wears a large gem pendant necklace at the neck of his tight black T-shirt and oversize black sunglasses perched on his smoothly shaved head. He has the bearing of a club DJ or a featherweight boxer. Before finding his true calling, he was a private investigator.

"I wasn't enjoying my work," he says. "So an old friend asked me to take a look at his ramen shop. I saw that for 500 yen people could be happy. So I became an apprentice for five years to learn to make ramen."

Eventually he opened his own shop, but soon realized he could no longer enjoy ramen: the MSG, he felt, was making him sick.

> # Ramen here has nearly nothing in common with the denatured supermarket variant. Real ramen knocks you back a little and then sets you right on your feet.

"It took me a year to create my own ramen without MSG, a year of studying dashi and making my own soy sauce to get the balance right."

The noodles at Genei are made in-house daily. They're springy, with a nice bit of chewiness due to an unusually high water content. Irie-san demonstrates his method of getting them just right: "I love you," he says, smacking a handful of noodles against the counter, gently squeezing and rolling them together, then pulling them apart and shaking them out again. The noodles now are curlier. "No stress," he says.

"I love you." Smack. "I love you...."

Shinji and I order a classic *tonkotsu* and another girded with shrimp oil. Each is finished with thin seared slices of pork, sliced *negi* (large Japanese scallion), and a plethora of greens. Irie-san's *tare* is the result of his yearlong quest to replace MSG with an

Preparing noodles
for soup at
Shifuku (429).

umami oomph of his own devising. In addition to the proprietary shoyu, or soy sauce (which he says costs him nearly $200 a liter), the *tare* incorporates kombu, bonito, a special sardine called *irune,* mackerel, dried shrimp, dried scallop, and dried abalone.

Activated by this blend, the soup is slightly frothy, the flavor massive, deeply, envelopingly meaty, but clean. Despite or perhaps because of its innovations, it's everything you'd want from an ideal *tonkotsu.* Everything but the traditional telltale brow-wrinkling stink.

Irie simmers his broth for 20 hours using only the bones from the heads of pigs. Pigs' heads, it turns out, smell sweet.

Shaping dough into noodles at Shifuku (429). Below: "Ramen Genovese" with green pesto at Ramen Unari, in Fukuoka.

KURUME TRAIN STATION
2 p.m. Kurume, 25 miles south of Fukuoka

The Bridgestone tire company was founded in this midsize industrial city on the Chikugo River in the 1930's. Outside the central train station, between the taxi queue and the parking structure, there is a monument to another of the city's claims to history.

The bronze statue is shaped like a *yatai,* an old-style street-food cart popular in this region and found nowhere else in Japan. Erected by the local Committee of Ramen Renaissance, the statue marks two signal moments in the development of *tonkotsu* ramen and the establishment of the region's preeminence in the evolution of noodle soup.

The short but complex story here is that in 1937, a gentleman from Kurume went to Yokohama and found in the stalls of Chinatown a noodle broth made of chicken bones. He had a hunch that pork bones would be even tastier, and opened a *yatai* called Nankin Senryo, thus establishing the local craze for ramen.

A few years later, another *yatai* owner's mother left a pot on the fire for too long. The overcooked soup turned creamy, cloudy, thick. Traditional Japanese dashi-based broths are valued for their clarity. This was something else altogether. But it was good, and from this happy accident the long-cooked Kyushu variant was born.

After paying our respects by the station, Shinji and I board a short local train called the Yellow One-Man Diesel Car. In a sleepy village a few stops away, the original Nankin Senryo still stands. Here, Miyamoto

Chieko, the daughter-in-law of the originator of the *tonkotsu* style, makes soup every day with her sons. Despite the global export of ramen, despite the vogue for new styles, the family hasn't changed the recipe in 75 years.

On the train ride home, Shinji and I read through a whole issue of *Ramen Walker* magazine. I am pretty sure none of this is a soup-induced dream. It all really happened.

YATAI NAGAHAMAYA #1
1 a.m. Nagahama District, Fukuoka City

Shinji and I are joined by some friends of friends, reporters at the local paper whom we got to know over a pre-ramen yakitori feast and several rounds of beer and sake. The reporters guide us to Nagahama, a neighborhood known for its distinct but hard-to-define style of ramen. Ganso Nagahamaya, a famous local shop, doesn't look like a restaurant; it looks like the loading bay of a factory. And it runs like an industrial operation for getting noodles and soup into mouths as efficiently as possible. Buy a ticket from the machine, and by the time you find a seat at one of the communal tables in the brightly lit space half open to the night air, the bowl is already in front of you. Nagahama style is lighter, the broth a little sour and salty, the noodles very thin and hard, the meat boiled and slight. It is not an immediately alluring bowl, but there is

something about it that makes you want more. One of the reporters claims to be on a diet. He finishes his bowl in two minutes. The other, a confirmed Ganso-phile, explains, "There is nothing special about this place but I find myself thinking about it always. Not because it's so tasty but because I am addicted. It can't be explained. Like love."

The addicted reporter estimates he's been here 200 times, and he can't stop coming back. We pat him on the back and tell him we understand.

From Ganso we walk to a nearby street lined with *yatai*. *Yatai* are miniature mobile restaurants. In the evenings they're unpacked for dinner business at the side of a canal or on certain blocks where they're licensed to operate in little clusters. The late drinking and snacking hours of the morning are the busiest; before sunrise, the *yatai* will be folded up and rolled out of sight. Each is no bigger than the kind of cart that would sell sunglasses in an American mall, but unfurled, they're somehow big enough to sit six or eight tightly around a little bar.

Japan doesn't have a culture of street food, so there is something festive and liberating about ducking into a *yatai*. It's like entering a compact, self-contained, jovial private-party-in-progress.

At Yatai Nagahamaya #1 we order a lot of *shochu* on the rocks, some *oden* (braised vegetables and gooey-textured fish-cake things bathing in broth) and a final bowl of rustic ramen. The dieting reporter finishes his without incident.

Ramen as a form is like the *yatai*: a space where the Japanese can go off script, cut loose, relax. The allure is that it's different at every place. We had our fill of textbook *tonkotsu* as well as tweaked modern varieties (such as green-pesto "Ramen Genovese" at the excellent little hipster shop Ramen Unari).

At Shifuku (429), we meet Sakimukai Yoshinobu, a hardworking dude whose riff is chicken *tonkotsu*: intensely yellow, luxuriously fatty stuff that may be the best chicken noodle soup in the world. Here is something new and old, another thing to dream about.

Shinji and I have been eating ramen for days. Every night, full of noodles, I think: no more. Then morning comes, lunchtime looms, and I relent: let's go for a bowl. ✦

GUIDE

EAT

Ganso Nagahamaya
2-5-19 Nagahama, Chuo-ku, Fukuoka; 81-92/781-0723. **$**

Ichiran Nakasu
5-3-2 Nakasu, Hakata-ku, Fukuoka; 81-92/262-0433. **$**

Mengekijo Genei
2-16-3 Yakuin, Chuo-ku, Fukuoka; 81-92/732-6100. **$**

Nankin Senryo
702-2 Nonakamachi, Kurume; 81-94/237-7279. **$**

Papapapapine
3-12-1 Nishi-Ogikubo,

Suginami-ku, Tokyo; papapapapine.com. **$**

Ramen Unari
6-23 Nakasu, Hakata-ku, Fukuoka; 81-92/281-8278. **$**

Shifuku (429)
2-3-1 Enokida, Hakata-ku, Fukuoka; 81-92/4740-0900. **$**

Tanaka Shoten
2-14-6 Hitotsuya, Adachi-ku, Tokyo; tanaka-shoten.net. **$**

Yatai Nagahamaya #1
1-10 Minato, Chuo-ku, Fukuoka. **$**

Sydney

Part outsize beach resort, part culture capital, Sydney has always exemplified the art of relaxed urbanity: cool but not pretentious; cutting-edge but laid-back. Now a new breed of local chefs are channeling that Aussie energy, blending a native farm-to-table ethos with global inspiration and reaffirming the city as one of the world's most exciting places to eat.

The Apollo

Australian chef Jonathan Barthelmess and owner Sam Christie teamed up to pay homage to their shared Greek heritage at this concrete-walled dining room in bohemian Potts Point. Updated taverna classics are the standard: try the smoky pita with onion-infused taramasalata (caviar dip), followed by the pickled octopus. A slice of the ouzo-soaked watermelon is the perfect way to top off the meal.
44 Macleay St.; 61-2/8354-0888; theapollo.com.au. **$$$**

The Bourbon

A pocket of New Orleans in the land down under? That's what you'll find at the Bourbon. The Creole menu hits all the right notes, from the Cajun-spiced pumpkin-and-okra lasagna to smoky jambalaya and popcorn-shrimp po'boys. A live jazz band and inventive drinks complete the picture; be sure to order the house cider, made with—what else?—bourbon, plus maple syrup and fresh purple basil.
22 Darlinghurst Rd.; 61-2/9035-8888; thebourbon.com.au. **$$$**

Chiswick

Matt Moran, Australia's answer to Anthony Bourdain, draws well-heeled diners to his rustic, light-filled dining room in the eastern suburb of Woollahra. Inside, long communal tables and rows of stacked firewood set the scene for an eclectic paddock-to-plate menu: orecchiette with chorizo and broccolini from the on-site garden, crisp buttermilk chicken with chile slaw and mango chutney, and wood-roasted lamb (sourced from the Moran family farm) with green olives and fennel. Caveat: tables fill up quickly, so make a reservation at least two weeks in advance.
65 Ocean St.; 61-2/8388-8688; chiswickrestaurant.com.au. **$$$**

Mr. Wong

Blink and you might miss this temple to upmarket Cantonese in a nondescript back alley in the Central Business District. An ode to 1930's Shanghai, the spacious restaurant spans two timber-floored levels; industrial-style lamps and ceiling fans hang above bamboo-framed chairs, and shelves are lined with antique teapots and vases. In the kitchen, chefs Dan Hong and Jowett Yu whip up flavorful dishes such as soy-and-ginger mud crab and honey-glazed *char siu* pork, while Erik Koh, an alum of London's renowned Hakkasan, oversees the dim sum. Don't leave without sampling his chicken-and-abalone dumplings.
3 Bridge Lane; 61-2/9240-3000; merivale.com. **$$$$**

Neild Avenue

On weekends, Sydney's fashion crowd heads to Neild Avenue, a former tire factory in Rushcutters Bay that was transformed into an avant-garde gastropub by Italian-Australian design duo Lazzarini Pickering (think multicolored murals, untreated wood, and polished concrete floors). Here, Mediterranean-inspired dishes are served family-style. Try the crisp four-cheese *arancini* (deep-fried rice balls) and the warm cheese-and-date tart, made with ricotta and cottage cheeses from Greece.
10 Neild Ave.; 61-2/8353-4400; neildavenue.com.au. **$$$**

Porteño and Gardel's Bar

Chefs Ben Milgate and Elvis Abrahanowicz's Argentinean grill house specializes in authentic *asado* (barbecue) that would make any gaucho proud. The meat-heavy menu includes beef-stuffed empanadas, chile-and-garlic blood sausage, and pig roasted over a rosewood fire pit—all served by a young, tattooed waitstaff. At night, the cocktail cognoscenti head upstairs to Gardel's Bar, a vintage-style supper club with leather booths and leopard-skin throws. Ask for a Fernet with cola and chance a game on the 1940's foosball table.
358 Cleveland St.; 61-2/8399-1440; porteno.com.au. **$$**

Reuben Hills

If it's hard to decide what time of day to visit Reuben Hills, a South American–inspired café in the industrial backstreets of Surry Hills, no worries. The restaurant features the same menu from morning until night. Come early for a breakfast of brioche with *dulce de leche* and Honduran *baleadas* (tortillas filled with eggs, black beans, and *queso fresco*); your flat-white coffee is made with beans from Panama's popular Hacienda La Esmeralda. Or stop by at dinnertime for the crab tacos with sweet corn and smoked tomatoes. Of course, you could also do it the other way around.
61 Albion St.; 61-2/9211-5556; reubenhills.com.au. **$$**

Chiswick's *vitello tonnato* sliders. Right: Mixing it up at Gardel's Bar, in Surry Hills.

Wok-fried mud crab from Mr. Wong. Left: A light installation at Reuben Hills.

asia+australia

A lunchtime crowd at Hobart's Garagistes. Opposite: Hapuku fish with dune spinach from the Stackings at Peppermint Bay, in Woodbridge.

Homegrown
Tasmania

BY JAY CHESHES / PHOTOGRAPHED BY EARL CARTER

Known for its wild beauty, Australia's southernmost state of Tasmania supplies some of the country's finest ingredients—from apples to abalone. Recently, however, the remote and rugged island has also become a playground for young, food-mad chefs from Sydney and Melbourne, who are striving to keep the remarkable bounty closer to home by heading up kitchens in and around the capital. The result? This rough-around-the-edges destination with a real pioneer vibe is suddenly brimming with good things to eat.

The Cultural Table

Just a 15-minute drive from Hobart, the Museum of Old & New Art may be the big news out of Tassie, but the Source Restaurant—housed in MONA's glass-wrapped upstairs pavilion—is making headlines of its own. Chef Philippe Leban, who was born in Brittany and raised in Sydney, draws on locavore-friendly ingredients to create the region's most refined dishes (roasted duck in coffee sauce; oysters from Bruny Island served with spanner crab meat, foie gras, and Pedro Ximénez sherry gelée), all set against a stunning Derwent River backdrop. He also grows his own herbs and produce in the restaurant's garden. On your way out, pick up a few bottles of Moorilla wine, made on site by Canadian vintner Conor van der Reest. The winery, one of Tasmania's oldest, produces dynamic cuvées with art-themed labels on every bottle. Then retire to one of the geometric, glass-and-steel guest pavilions located on MONA's grounds.

The Dessert Emporium

If there's one vexing problem with husband-and-wife team Alistair Wise and Teena Kearney-Wise's diminutive spot in North Hobart, it's the "What do I order?" paralysis it inspires as you walk in the door. Before you can decide between Sweet Envy's salted caramels, Montélimar nougat, chocolate bonbons, and lemon-meringue doughnuts, a young salesgirl may dare you to take the "cupcake challenge"—devour it in 60 seconds or less, and the peanut-butter-frosted concoction is free (it doesn't seem particularly difficult until you hear about the "no-hands" stipulation). Alistair, a Tasmanian native who worked as a pastry chef at Gordon Ramsay at the London, in New York City, uses fresh fruit to concoct Willy Wonka–esque ice cream flavors such as white nectarine and tarragon, blood plum and yogurt, and *cajeta* (a syrup made with goat's milk and sugar, similar to *dulce de leche*) with strawberries. On the go? Keep an eye out for the ice cream truck outside, a 1964 Commer Karrier named Big Bessie that the couple restored themselves.

Crisp blood sausage and pickled egg from the New Sydney Hotel. Left: A John Olsen ceiling mural at the Source.

The Destination Lunch Spot

Don't bother renting a car. In just 1½ hours, a 75-foot catamaran can take you down the coast from Hobart to the Stackings at Peppermint Bay, a soaring metal-and-glass gastro-temple in nearby Woodbridge. Chef David Moyle enthusiastically embraces the foraging zeitgeist with three- and five-course lunch menus that are improvised daily, highlighting whatever is at its peak: sea lettuce that Moyle plucked from the shoreline, tart Kentish Red cherries from the trees of a friend, or wild garlic gathered along country roads.

The Gastropub

Crowded with a rotating cast of regulars nursing their pints, the New Sydney Hotel is a working-class pub in Hobart that dates from 1835. But across from the beer signs and dinged license plates is a blackboard that reveals 21st-century offerings. Chef John Wiseman stocks his menu with dishes of Spanish-style blood sausage accompanied by a red-onion aioli, crisp goat shoulder with chickpeas, pumpkin, and watercress,

and lamb breast with almonds and mint. Sometimes you'll find local game (possum and wallaby) and, in winter, bowls of risotto with shaved Tasmanian truffles. Try one of the restaurant's infused beers, such as the spiced porter with ginger and chiles, made using the region's first "hopinator," an oddball brewing contraption.

The Haute Farm Stand

If there's a poster child for Tasmania's new food pilgrims, Matthew Evans is it. In 2005, he retired from his position as a restaurant critic for the *Sydney Morning Herald* and moved to the island, determined to learn farming. His *Green Acres*–style experiment, chronicled in books and on the Australian reality show *Gourmet Farmer*, gave rise to A Common Ground, a tiny shop near Hobart's waterfront. Every square inch of shelf and floor space is devoted to made-in-Tasmania products—pickled walnuts, bespoke chocolate bars, truffled honey, and saffron. Handmade sausages and rillettes (some from pigs Evans reared himself) sit

The glass-walled dining room at the Stackings at Peppermint Bay.

alongside cheeses created by Nick Haddow, a partner in the store and owner of the Bruny Island Cheese Company; ask for a sample of the intense Raw Milk C2. In keeping with the local focus, the shop hosts long-table lunches in the countryside—in a paddock, say, or a potato field—where diners are often joined by the farmers who grew their food.

The Urban Wine Bar
Judging by its black-clad kitchen brigade and industrial-loft vibe, Garagistes could be a burgeoning hot spot in New York or London. A haunch of ham and other artisanal salumi hang in a showcase cooler; the modern wooden furniture was made by area craftsmen. The perennially packed Hobart restaurant takes its name from its setting: an airy converted Volkswagen garage with scuffed brick, exposed beams, and an open kitchen that overlooks rows of communal tables in the dining room. Here, chef Luke Burgess, a former food and travel photographer, prepares dishes that are complex and obsessively local. The wood-roasted Wagyu beef—which melts on the tongue—with apples and garlic comes from cattle grass-fed on a small island off Tassie's northwestern coast. The parsnips, served with chestnuts and a prickly-pear granita, are in the ground just hours before they show up on your plate. If you can't snag a seat right away (which is often the case), wait it out at Sidecar, a cozy annex bar that Burgess and his partners opened to help ease the restaurant's nightly bottleneck. ✚

GUIDE

EAT
A Common Ground Shop
3 Salamanca Arts Centre,
77 Salamanca Place, Hobart;
61-4/2937-0192;
acommonground.com. **$$$**

Garagistes
103 Murray St., Hobart;
61-3/6231-0558;
garagistes.com.au. **$$$**

New Sydney Hotel
87 Bathurst St., Hobart;
61-3/6234-4516;
newsydneyhotel.com.au. **$$$**

Source Restaurant
655 Main Rd., Berriedale;
61-3/6277-9904;
mona.net.au. **$$$$**

Stackings at
Peppermint Bay
3435 Channel Hwy.,
Woodbridge;
61-3/6267-4088;
peppermintbay.com.au. **$$$**

Sweet Envy
341 Elizabeth St.,
North Hobart; 61-3/6234-
8805; sweetenvy.com. **$**

Oysters on the
half shell at
Contramar, in
Mexico City.

Contributors

WRITERS

Colin Barraclough

Anya von Bremzen

Jennifer Chen

Jay Cheshes

Mark Ellwood

Peter J. Frank

David Lebovitz

Matt Lee and Ted Lee

Peter Jon Lindberg

Alexandra Marshall

Shane Mitchell

Douglas Rogers

Adam Sachs

Bruce Schoenfeld

Gary Shteyngart

Daniel Vaughn

PHOTOGRAPHERS

Jessica Antola 6, 88, 113 (bottom right)

Alex Arnold 21 (bottom left)

Daniel Boud 183 (top; bottom right)

Stefano Buonamici/ New York Times/Redux 101 (top left)

Felix Busso 77 (top right)

Brown W. Cannon III/ Intersection Photos 158, 160-171

Earl Carter 184-189, 192

Tara Donne 58-65, 68-75

DOOK 138, 140 (top right, bottom), 143, 146, 147 (left)

Alex Farnum 34-45

Amanda Friedman 47 (top left)

Luis Garcia 8, 56, 67, 190

Kristin Gladney 125 (top left, bottom)

Andres Gonzalez 125 (top right)

Emiliano Granado 21 (bottom right)

Marie Hennechart 113 (left)

Jody Horton 33 (top right)

Gunnar Knechtal 101 (bottom left)

Yadid Levy 77 (top left)

Jason Lowe 90-99

Mark Mahaney 2-3, 10, 12-18

Nicholas McWhirter 33 (bottom right)

Tetsuya Miura 174-180

David Nicolas 78-87

Marcus Nilsson 102-111, 136, 149

Javier Pierini 77 (bottom right)

Andrew Rowat 173 (left)

Baerbel Schmidt 150-157

Dagmar Schwelle 126-135

Evan Sung 21 (top right)

Christopher Testani 21 (top left)

Petrina Tinslay 183 (bottom left)

Richard Truscott 113 (top right)

Coral Von Zumwalt 5, 22-30, 47 (bottom), 48-55

Christopher Wise 173 (right)

Andrea Wyner 114-122

FRAMBOISE
6·8

CHUNKY
MONKEY
6·8

Pastries at
North Hobart's
Sweet Envy,
in Tasmania,
Australia.

MELBA
8·5

ODE TO......
VANILLA SLICE
6·8

THE NUTTY
CHOUX
6·8

BANO

CHEESECAKE
8·5

LEMON
CURD
4

CHOCOLATE
SALTY CARAMEL
4·5